RON KALENUIK

The Original Pizza & Pasta Cookbook

SIMPLY DELICIOUS
COOKING SERIES™

MAGNANIMITY
HOUSE PUBLISHING

Credits

Project Coordinator :	Dianna Kalenuik
Editor :	Sharon Antoniuk
Cuisine Coordinator :	Chef Ron Kalenuik
Cuisine Assistants :	Pamela Kalenuik Timothy Kalenuik Jennifer Kalenuik Ruth Maier
Art Direction :	Sylvia Cook
Photography :	V.E.T. Marketing
Design / Graphic / PrePress :	Sako Graphics Resource Centre Inc.

© Magnanimity House Publishers
Box 97509
Highland Creek, P.O.
Scarborough, ON. Canada, M1C 4Z1
Telephone 416-724-7287
Fax 416-724-7857

This book is an Exclusive Edition for

250 Granton Dr.
Richmond Hill ON. L4B 1H7
714-587-9207
Printed in the United States of America

Contents

Pizza

Take a piece of pan bread, top it with a little sauce and a few other ingredients from meat to cheese, and see it sweep the world off its feet. Such is the history and reputation of the pizza.

In France they call it pissaladière, in the Middle East it's a pita, in Mexico it is a tortilla topped with great delights. In essence, a pizza is nothing more than a baked, opened-faced sandwich, but what a sandwich!

The pizza is believed to be a culinary invention from Naples, Italy (home of that other popular Italian food, spaghetti). First called the Pizze

Napoletana Verace, (the true Neapolitan pizza) originally consisted of a base of pan type brea tomato, garlic, olive oil and oregano baked in hot oven and sold on the street. The addition cheese came some time later and with it cam the first culinary free-for-all. Soon, no matter what ingredient, one had put it on a pizza and you were well on your way to success. Pizza has sustained the poverty-ridden (as in the po street people of Italy) and entertained the wel to-do (as it does in Wolfgang Puck's restauran to the stars, Spago).

One may be assured of one thing, with pizza,

...sual entertaining will always be fun, exciting ...d not expensive. Pizza has become the food ...unify friendships forever. Every nationality ...joys good fellowship and intimate ...mpanionship around this most influential of ...cuisines.

...zza may come disguised as a calzone or a ...nzarotti (a sort of pizza turnover) or a double-...usted pie with the filling completely enclosed. ...ithin the pages of this chapter you may look ...rward to a selection of pizzas that will delight ...ends and family for years to come. Each is an ...ginal creation of excitement, which is exactly

what will take place when your guests sample their first bite, utter excitement, coupled with the cry for more.

You may sample such delights as a Greek Isle Pizza, or the Potato Chicken Calzone or plan some intrigue with our Jamaican Jerk Chicken Pizza. Why you may even entertain with dessert pizzas or, create your own. All the basic recipes for creative pizzas are found within these pages. The final result of the party you host will be the happy guest and their determined inquisition of gaining your recipes.

Milano Pizza

Ingredients:

1 lb	454 g	grocer purchased Basic Pizza Dough or 1 quantity of our recipe
1 cup	250 ml	Pizza Sauce (see page 14)
1 lb	454 g	hot Italian sausage, diced and cooked
12 oz	340 g	diced Mozzarella cheese
1½ cups	375 ml	sliced roasted red peppers
1½ cups	375 ml	sliced Vidalia onion

Preparation:

Pan the dough as per instructions. Sauce the pizza and top with the sausage.

Sprinkle with the cheese, top with the red peppers and onions.

Bake in a preheated 450°F (230°C) oven for 10-12 minutes or until golden brown.

YIELDS two 12" (30 cm) pizzas.

Basic Pizza Dough

Ingredients:

1 tsp	5 ml	granulated sugar
1 cup	250 ml	warm water
1 tbsp	15 ml	(envelope) of active dry yeast
2 tbsp	30 ml	butter, melted and cooled
3½ cups	875 ml	all purpose flour
⅛ tsp	pinch	salt

Preparation:

In a large bowl, dissolve the sugar in the warm water. Sprinkle with the yeast and let stand 10 minutes or until foamy. Stir in the butter.

Stir in half the flour and a pinch of salt into the yeast mixture. Gradually stir in enough of the remaining flour to make a slightly sticky ball.

Knead the dough on a lightly floured surface until smooth and elastic, about 5 minutes.

Place the dough into a greased bowl and let rest 15 minutes. Punch down the dough; cut in half. Roll out each piece of dough into an 11" (28 cm) circle, allow to rise again, 15 minutes.

Place on a greased 14" (35 cm) pizza pan. With finger tips press the dough from centre towards the edge until half the pan is covered, rest the dough for 10 minutes. Press once again until the dough covers the pan completely.

Dough is now ready for sauce and toppings.

Barbecue Chicken Pizza

DOUGH:

Ingredients:

2 tbsp	30 ml	dry active yeast
¼ cup	60 ml	warm water
2½ cups	625 ml	unbleached flour
1 tsp	5 ml	salt
⅓ cup	80 ml	olive oil
2	2	eggs

Preparation:

In a large mixing bowl, dissolve the yeast in the water, let it rest 10 minutes. Add 1 cup (250 ml) of flour, the salt and oil. Beat into a smooth batter. Add ½ cup (125 ml) of the flour and the eggs, blend thoroughly.

Turn out onto a floured surface. Knead and gradually add the remaining flour, knead into a smooth ball.

Place into a greased bowl, cover and allow to rise for 1½ hours. Punch down and divide into two. Roll dough into rounds and place into two 8"(20 cm) pans. Dough is now ready for sauce and topping.

SAUCE:

Ingredients:

3 tbsp	45 ml	olive oil
2 tbsp	30 ml	minced onion
2 tbsp	30 ml	minced green peppers
2 tbsp	30 ml	minced celery
1	1	minced garlic clove
¼ cup	60 ml	white wine
¼ tsp	1 ml	black pepper
½ tsp	3 ml	oregano leaves
½ tsp	3 ml	ground cumin
3 tbsp	45 ml	brown sugar
1¼ cups	310 ml	tomato pureé
½ tsp	3 ml	hickory smoked salt

Preparation:

Heat the oil in a saucepan. Add the onion, green peppers, celery and garlic, sauté until tender. Blend in the remaining ingredients. Bring the sauce to a boil, reduce heat and simmer for 20 minutes.

TOPPING:

Ingredients:

2 tbsp	30 ml	olive oil
1	1	minced garlic clove
1 lb	454 ml	sliced, boneless skinless chicken breast
8 oz	225 g	grated smoked Gouda cheese
¼ cup	60 ml	sliced black olive

Preparation:

Pour the oil into a mixing bowl, add the garlic and chicken, toss to coat the chicken. Sauté the chicken in a large skillet.

Spread the dough evenly with the sauce, top with chicken. Sprinkle with the cheese and olives.

Bake in a preheated 450°F (230°C) oven for 15 minutes or until golden brown. Remove from the oven, slice and serve.

YIELDS two 8" (20 cm) pizzas

Chef's Corner

Dicing Onions

The best method of dicing an onion is to first cut along the grain from the blossom end to the root. Remove the skin. Cut away the root end as this is bitter and woody tasting. Cut the onion in half from the blossom end to the root. Cut the onion once again in the opposite direction but not completely through. Cut the onion in as many slices as you desire ⅛" (3 mm) from the blossom end to the root. Cut in the opposite direction into a dice. The more slits and cuts placed in the onion will result in a finer dice.

Greek Isles Pizza

Ingredients:

¾ lb	345 g	boneless lamb
1 tsp	5 ml	salt
1 tbsp	15 ml	oregano
½ tsp	3 ml	garlic powder
1 tsp	5 ml	Worcestershire sauce
3 tbsp	45 ml	lemon juice
⅓ cup	80 ml	olive oil
½ lb	225 g	grocer purchased Herb Pizza Dough or ½ quantity of our recipe (see page 38)
1	1	julienne-cut red bell pepper
1	1	diced onion
3 oz	80 g	sliced, sautéed mushrooms
5 oz	150 g	julienne-cut sun-dried tomatoes rehydrated
1½ cups	375 ml	grated Mozzarella cheese
1½ cups	375 ml	crumbled Feta cheese

Preparation:

Slice the lamb into thin strips and place in a mixing bowl. Blend in the salt, oregano, garlic powder, Worcestershire sauce, lemon juice and half the oil. Cover and marinate for 2 hours. Drain.

Heat the remaining oil in a skillet and quickly fry the lamb. Cool.

Pan the dough according to instructions. Preheat the oven to 450°F (230°C).

Spoon over the dough, the lamb, peppers, onions, mushrooms and tomatoes. Cover with the cheese. Bake for 15 minutes or until golden brown. Remove from the pan, slice and serve.

YIELDS two 8" (20 cm) or one 12" (30 cm) pizza

Seafood Lovers Dream

Ingredients:

¾ lb	345 g	diced lobster meat
¾ lb	345 g	scallops
¾ lb	345 g	large peeled and de-veined shrimp
4 cups	1 L	seafood or chicken broth (see page 146)
2 tbsp	30 ml	butter
4 oz	120 g	sliced mushrooms
1	1	finely diced onion
2 cups	500 ml	Mornay Sauce
1 lb	454 g	grocer purchased Whole Wheat Pizza Dough or 1 quantity of our recipe (see page 18) or Herb Dough (see page 38)
2 tbsp	30 ml	olive oil
2 cups	500 ml	grated Havarti cheese
¾ cup	180 ml	Béarnaise Sauce

Preparation:

Cook the lobster, scallops and shrimp in the court bouillon. (Do not over-cook to prevent seafood from becoming tough). Drain and cool.

Heat the butter in a saucepan. Sauté the mushrooms and onions until tender.
Add the Mornay Sauce and simmer until sauce thickens.

Preheat the oven to 450°F (230°C). Pan the crust according to instructions. Brush with oil. Spread with the seafood, then with the Mornay Sauce. Sprinkle with the cheese.

Bake 12 minutes. Cover with the Béarnaise Sauce and continue to bake for an additional 3-5 minutes or until sauce browns nicely.

Remove from the pan, slice and serve.

YIELDS four 8" (20 cm) or two 12" (30 cm) pizzas.

Béarnaise Sauce

Ingredients:

3 tbsp	45 ml	white wine
1 tbsp	15 ml	dried tarragon leaves
1 tsp	5 ml	lemon juice
½ cup	125 ml	butter
3	3	egg yolks
1 tsp	5 ml	fresh chopped tarragon

Preparation:

Combine the wine, tarragon and lemon juice in a small pan. Over high heat reduce to 2 tbsp (30 ml), then strain.

In another small saucepan, melt the butter and heat to almost boiling.

In a blender or food processor, process the egg yolks until blended.

With the machine running, add the butter in a slow thin stream.

With the machine on slow, add the reduced wine mixture. Process just until blended. Place in a serving bowl. Stir in the fresh tarragon.

YIELDS ¾ cup (180 ml)

Mornay Sauce

Ingredients:

3 tbsp	45 ml	butter
3 tbsp	45 ml	flour
1¼ cups	310 ml	chicken broth (see page 146)
1¼ cups	310 ml	half & half cream
½ cup	125 ml	freshly grated Parmesan cheese

Preparation:

Heat the butter in a saucepan. Add the flour and cook 2 minutes over low heat. Stir in the chicken broth and cream. Reduce heat and simmer until thickened. Stir in the cheese and simmer for 2 more minutes.

Use as required.

YIELDS 3 cups (750 ml)

Vancouver Crab
and Vegetable Pizza

Ingredients:

1 lb	454 g	grocer purchased Whole Wheat Pizza Dough or ½ quantity of our recipe (see page 18)
¾ cup	180 ml	Pizza Sauce
2 cups	500 ml	diced, cooked crab meat
1 cup	250 ml	shredded Monterey Jack cheese
5 oz	150 g	chopped spinach
¼ cup	60 ml	sliced black olives
½ cup	125 ml	sliced red onion
½ cup	125 ml	sliced marinated artichoke hearts, drained
3	3	Roma tomatoes, sliced into rounds
1 cup	250 ml	crumbled Feta cheese
1 tsp	5 ml	dried oregano

Preparation:

Process the dough according to the directions.

Preheat the oven to 450°F (230°C).

Pan the dough into a 12" (30 cm) pizza pan.

Spread the Pizza Sauce evenly on the prepared pizza dough. Top with the crab meat. Add the Monterey Jack cheese and top with the spinach. Top with the olives, onions, artichoke hearts and sliced tomatoes.

Top with the Feta cheese and sprinkle with the oregano.

Bake for 12-15 minutes or until golden brown, remove from the oven, slice and serve.

YIELDS one 12" (30 cm) pizza

Pizza Sauce

Ingredients:

3 tbsp	45 ml	vegetable or olive oil
2	2	minced garlic cloves
1	1	finely diced onion
1	1	finely diced celery stalk
½	0.5	finely diced green bell pepper
3 lbs	1.3 kg	peeled, seeded and chopped tomatoes
1 tsp	5 ml	dried oregano leaves
1 tsp	5 ml	dried thyme leaves
1 tsp	5 ml	dried basil leaves
1 tsp	5 ml	salt
½ tsp	3 ml	cracked black pepper
1 tbsp	15 ml	Worcestershire sauce
⅔ cup	160 ml	tomato paste

Preparation:

In a large pot, heat the oil. Sauté the vegetables until tender. Add the tomatoes, seasonings, Worcestershire sauce and tomato paste. Reduce heat and simmer for 2 hours, or until sauce is very thick, stirring occasionally. Cool.

YIELDS 2 cups (500 ML)

Eggs Benedict Pizza

Ingredients:

1 lb	454 g	grocer purchased Basic Pizza Dough or ½ quantity of our recipe (see page 6)
2 tbsp	30 ml	olive oil
½ tsp	3 ml	dried thyme leaves
½ tsp	3 ml	dried basil leaves
½ tsp	3 ml	dried oregano leaves
4 oz	115 g	grated Pecorino or Caciocavallo cheese
½ cup	125 ml	butter
2	2	egg yolks
2 tsp	10 ml	lemon juice
⅛ tsp	pinch	cayenne pepper
9	9	eggs
16	16	slices Canadian bacon
2 tbsp	30 ml	red caviar
2 tbsp	30 ml	black caviar
		parsley for garnish

Preparation:

Preheat the oven to 450°F (230°C).

Prepare the dough according to the directions. Pan the dough into a 12" (30 cm) pizza pan. Brush the dough with the olive oil. Sprinkle with the thyme, basil and oregano leaves. Bake in the oven for 8 minutes. Sprinkle with the cheese and continue to bake to golden brown.

While the dough bakes, melt the butter to very hot. Remove dough from the oven.

Turn the oven to broil.

Place the egg yolks in a double boiler over low heat.

Add the lemon juice slowly, be sure its thoroughly incorporated.

Remove from the heat, slowly whisk in the hot butter. Add the cayenne.

Poach the eggs in an egg poacher.

Top the dough with slices of the bacon, place the eggs around the dough equally. Smother each egg with the sauce. Place the pizza under the oven broiler and bake until golden brown.

Remove from the oven and garnish each egg with the caviars and parsley. Serve at once.

YIELDS one 12" (30 cm) pizza

Grilled Shrimp Pizza
with Red Pepper Pesto

Ingredients:

1 lb	454 g	grocer purchased Whole Wheat Pizza Dough or ½ quantity of our recipe
1 lb	454 g	large shrimp
2 tbsp	30 ml	olive oil
½ tsp	3 ml	each of salt, pepper, basil, paprika
2 cups	500 ml	shredded Mozzarella
2	2	large sliced tomatoes
½ cup	125 ml	sliced green onions

Pesto:

1	1	minced garlic clove
2 tbsp	30 ml	pine nuts
1 tbsp	15 ml	chopped fresh basil leaves
3 tbsp	45 ml	chopped parsley
1 cup	250 ml	seeded and diced red peppers
3 oz	90 g	freshly grated Romano cheese
¼ cup	60 ml	olive oil

Preparation:

Process the dough according to the directions.

Preheat the oven to 450°F (230°C).

Peel and de-vein the shrimp, place in a mixing bowl. Add the oil and seasonings, marinate for 20 minutes. Grill the shrimp for 3 minutes per side. Cool.

In a food processor, process the garlic and pine nuts until very fine. Add the basil, parsley, peppers, Romano cheese and process into a purée. Slowly add the oil and continue to process into a mayonnaise like sauce.

Pan the dough in a 12" (30 cm) pizza pan, top with the pesto, cheese and shrimp. Arrange the tomato slices on top and sprinkle with the green onions.

Bake for 12-15 minutes or until golden brown, remove, slice and serve.

YIELDS one 12" pizza

Whole Wheat Dough

Ingredients:

1 tbsp	15 ml	dry active yeast
¾ cup	180 ml	warm water
1 cup	250 ml	whole wheat pastry flour
1 ½ cups	375 ml	unbleached all purpose flour
1	1	egg, beaten
½ tsp	3 ml	salt
3 tbsp	45 ml	olive oil

Preparation:

In a large bowl, dissolve the yeast in the water. Let rest for 10 minutes or until foamy. Add the whole wheat flour, ½ cup (125 ml) unbleached flour, the egg, salt and oil and stir into a smooth paste.

Gradually knead in the remaining flour and continue to knead into a smooth ball.

Let the dough rise for 15 minutes. Divide in half. Roll each half into a round on a lightly floured surface.

Place each round into a lightly oiled pizza pan. Let rise 15 minutes longer. With your finger tips, press dough from centre to the edges until the pan is completely covered by dough.

Dough is now ready for the sauce and toppings.

YIELDS four 8" (20 cm) or two 12" (30 cm) pizzas

Sfinciuni
Double Stuffed Pizza

Ingredients:

½ cup	125 ml	finely chopped celery
⅓ cup	80 ml	chopped pimento-stuffed green olives
¼ cup	60 ml	chopped porcini mushrooms
¼ cup	60 ml	chopped cocktail onions
1	1	minced garlic clove
¼ cup	60 ml	extra virgin olive oil
2 tbsp	30 ml	balsamic vinegar
½ tsp	3 ml	salt
½ tsp	3 ml	pepper
½ tsp	3 ml	dried thyme leaves
½ tsp	3 ml	dried basil leaves
½ tsp	3 ml	dried oregano leaves
1 lb	454 g	grocer purchased Gourmet Pizza Dough or 1 quantity of our recipe
4 oz	115 g	prosciutto
8 oz	225 g	shredded Provolone cheese
		extra virgin olive oil for brushing

Preparation:

In a mixing bowl combine the celery, olives, mushrooms, onions, garlic, oil, vinegar and seasonings. Marinate for 1 ½ hours refrigerated.

Preheat the oven to 450°F (230°C).

Prepare the dough according to the directions, divide into two equal portions.

Pan half the dough into a 12" (30 cm) pizza pan. Top with the marinated vegetables, prosciutto and Provolone cheese. Roll out the second half of the dough and cover the first layer, crimp the edges to seal. Brush with the oil.

Bake in the oven for 30 minutes or until golden brown. Remove from the oven, slice and serve.

YIELDS one 12" (30 cm) pizza

Gourmet Dough

Ingredients:

2 tbsp	30 ml	granulated sugar
¼ cup	60 ml	warm water
2 tbsp	30 ml	dry active yeast
2 cups	500 ml	milk
1 tsp	5 ml	salt
3 tbsp	45 ml	butter
6½ cups	1.6 L	all purpose flour
1	1	egg, beaten
¼ cup	60 ml	heavy cream

Preparation:

Mix 1 tsp (5 ml) of sugar in the warm water. Dissolve the yeast in the water and let soften 10 minutes.

In a saucepan, combine the milk, remaining sugar, salt and butter. Scald, then cool. Transfer to a mixing bowl.

Stir in the yeast mixture and 3 cups (750 ml) of flour. Beat for 2 minutes. Cover. Allow to rise for 1 hour, then beat in the remaining flour, egg, and the heavy cream.

Knead in a mixer for 8 minutes. Cover and allow to rise.

Divide the dough evenly into either two or four and place onto well-greased pans (as required by your pizza recipe). Allow to rise for 15 minutes. Spread the dough evenly over the pans by pressing it out from the centre with your finger tips, covering the entire pan.

YIELDS four 8" (20 cm) or two 12" (30 cm) pizzas

Sicilian Pizza

Dough:
Ingredients:

2 tbsp	30 ml	dry active yeast
1 cup	250 ml	warm water
3½ cups	875 ml	unbleached flour approximately
4	4	minced garlic cloves
3 tbsp	45 ml	chopped chives
½ cup	125 ml	freshly grated Parmesan cheese
2	2	eggs, beaten
¼ cup	60 ml	olive oil

Preparation:

In a large mixing bowl dissolve the yeast in the warm water. Rest 10 minutes or until foamy. Stir in 2 cups (500 ml) of flour along with the garlic, chives, Parmesan, eggs and oil, forming a smooth batter.

Stir and knead in gradually the remaining flour or enough to form a smooth ball. Place into a greased bowl, cover and rest 15 minutes. Divide in two and roll into rounds on a lightly floured surface. Place into pans which have been lightly oiled. Rest 15 minutes. With finger tips press dough from centre out to cover the entire pan.

Dough is now ready for sauce and toppings.

Toppings:
Ingredients:

4 tbsp	60 ml	olive oil
1 lb	454 g	fresh plum tomatoes
3	3	minced garlic cloves
1 tbsp	15 ml	fresh basil chopped
½ tsp	3 ml	each of salt and pepper
8	8	marinated artichoke hearts, drained, quartered
8 oz	225 g	Prosciutto, cut julienne style
6 oz	170 g	diced Gorgonzola cheese
6 oz	170 g	grated Pecorino cheese
⅓ cup	80 ml	black olives, pitted and sliced
2	2	fresh large tomatoes, sliced

Preparation:

While the dough rises, heat 2 tbsp (30 ml) of the oil in a saucepan.

Peel and quarter the plum tomatoes. Add to the oil along with the garlic, basil, salt and pepper. Reduce the heat and simmer for 30 minutes.

Brush the remaining oil over the dough, spread with the sauce. Top with the artichoke hearts and prosciutto.

Sprinkle with the cheeses and top with the olives and tomatoes.

Bake in a preheated 450°F (230°C) oven for 10-12 minutes or until golden brown.

YIELDS two 8" (20 cm) pizzas.

Peach Melba Pizza

Ingredients:

¾ lb	345 g	peeled, stoned apricots
1 lb	454 g	fresh raspberries
½ cup	125 ml	apple juice
2 tbsp	30 ml	lemon juice
¼ cup	60 ml	sugar
2 lbs	900 g	grocer purchased Gourmet Pizza Dough or 1 quantity of our recipe (see page 20)
10	10	large peaches, peeled stoned and halved
2 cups	500 ml	cubed Bel Paese cheese

Preparation:

Place the apricots and raspberries in a food processor, purée. Press through a sieve (to remove seeds) into a sauce pan. Blend in the apple juice, lemon juice and sugar, simmer into a very thick sauce. Cool to room temperature.

Process the dough as per instructions.

While the dough is rising, blanch the peach halves in boiling sugar water for 5 minutes. Drain and cool.

Pan the dough as instructed for Gourmet Pizza Dough. Spread the dough with the raspberry sauce. Place peaches over the dough. Sprinkle with cheese and bake in a preheated 450°F (230°C) oven for 10-12 minutes or until golden brown.

Remove from pan, slice and serve.

YIELDS two 12" (30 cm) pizzas.

San Diego Pizza

Dough:

Ingredients:

2 tbsp	30 ml	dry active yeast (2 envelopes)
1½ cups	375 ml	warm water
4 cups	1 L	all purpose flour -approximately
1 tsp	5 ml	salt
½ tsp	3 ml	each of basil, thyme, black cracked pepper, red pepper flakes
¼ cup	60 ml	olive oil

Preparation:

In a large mixing bowl, dissolve the yeast in the warm water. Rest 10 minutes or until foamy.

Stir in 2 cups (500 ml) of flour along with the salt and seasonings. Stir into a smooth batter. Stir in the oil. Add 1 cup (250 ml) of flour mixing into a ball. Add enough flour to form a smooth dough. Dough should not be sticky.

Knead the dough for 5 minutes, and allow to rest 15 minutes. Divide into two. Roll out into 11" (28 cm) circles. Rest an additional 15 minutes. Place dough into 12" (30 cm) lightly oiled pizza pans. With your fingertips press dough from centre to the edges until pan is completely covered by dough.

Dough is now ready for sauce and toppings.

Toppings:

Ingredients:

3 tbsp	45 ml	herb-flavored olive oil
12 oz	340 g	boneless, diced chicken
12 oz	340 g	large shrimp, peeled and de-veined
1 cup	250 ml	Diego Sauce
24 oz	680 g	grated Mozzarella cheese
½ cup	125 ml	grated Parmesan cheese
8	8	marinated artichoke hearts, drained, quartered
1 cup	250 ml	oil preserved sundried tomatoes
1 cup	250 ml	blanched broccoli florets

Preparation:

Heat 2 tbsp (30 ml) of olive oil in a skillet. Sauté the chicken and shrimp until cooked through.

Brush the dough with the remaining oil.

Sauce the pizza with a ½ cup (125 ml) of sauce. Spread with the chicken and shrimp. Cover with equal amounts of the cheese. Top with the remaining ingredients.

Bake in a preheated 450°F (230°C) oven for 10-12 minutes or until golden brown.

YIELDS two 12" (30 cm) pizzas.

Diego Sauce:

Ingredients:

3	3	red cascabel chilies
⅓ cup	80 ml	olive oil
1	1	finely diced onion
2	2	minced garlic cloves
1½ lbs	675 g	peeled, seeded and chopped tomatoes
2 tsp	10 ml	oregano leaves

Preparation:

Seed and dice the chilies and mix with ½ the oil. Marinate for 1 hour.

Heat the remaining oil in a sauce pan. Sauté the onion and garlic until tender.

Drain the marinade and mix the chilies with the onion. Add the tomatoes and the oregano. Reduce heat to medium and simmer until sauce has thickened.

Use as required, balance may be kept refrigerated for up to 10 days.

Palm Springs Pizza

Dough:
Ingredients:

2 tbsp	30 ml	dry active yeast
¼ cup	60 ml	warm water
2¼ cups	560 ml	unbleached flour
1 tsp	5 ml	salt
⅓ cup	80 ml	olive oil
2	2	eggs, beaten

Preparation:

In a large mixing bowl, dissolve the yeast in the water, let it rest 10 minutes. Add 1 cup (250 ml) of flour, the salt and oil. Beat into a smooth batter. Add ½ cup (125 ml) of flour and the eggs, blend thoroughly.

Turn out onto a floured surface. Knead and gradually add the remaining flour, knead into a smooth ball.

Place into a greased bowl, cover and allow to rise for 1½ hours. Punch down. Roll the dough into a round and place into a pan which has been lightly oiled. Dough is now ready for topping.

Toppings:
Ingredients:

3 tbsp	45 ml	red pepper olive oil
12 oz	340 g	boneless diced chicken
½ cup	125 ml	Pizza Sauce (see page 14)
1 cup	250 ml	sliced Portobello mushrooms
1½ cups	375 ml	grated Cacciocavallo cheese
1½ cups	375 ml	grated Mozzarella cheese
½ cup	125 ml	roasted red bell peppers sliced

Preparation:

Heat 2 tbsp (30 ml) of the oil in a skillet. Sauté the chicken.

Brush the dough with the remaining oil.

Sauce each of the pizzas with a ¼ cup (60 ml) of the Pizza Sauce. Sprinkle the chicken and mushrooms over the pizza. Top with the cheeses and red bell peppers.

Bake in a preheated 450°F (230°C) oven for 10-12 minutes or until golden brown.

SERVES 6

Chef's Corner

Portobello Mushrooms

Portobello mushrooms are large umbrella shapes with a very rich earthy meaty flavor. Excellent in all cuisines. They can be used on their own as appetizers, stuffed or marinated and grilled.

Tucson Pizza

Ingredients:

3 tbsp	45 ml	olive oil
1 lb	454 g	hot Italian sausage
1	1	julienne cut leek
1	1	finely diced red bell pepper
2	2	finely diced jalapeño peppers
3 oz	80 g	sliced porcini mushrooms
1	1	minced garlic clove
½ tsp	3 ml	salt
¼ tsp	1 ml	each of basil, oregano, thyme, black pepper
1 cup	250 ml	Pizza Sauce (see page 14)
1 lb	454 g	grocer purchased Gourmet Pizza Dough or 1 quantity of our recipe (see page 20)
1 cup	250 ml	grated Mozzarella cheese
1 cup	250 ml	Bocconcini cheese
½ cup	125 ml	freshly grated Parmesan cheese
1	1	egg

Preparation:

In a large pot or Dutch oven, heat the oil and cook the sausage meat. Drain the excess fat. Add the vegetables and sauté until tender. Add the seasonings and Pizza Sauce. Reduce the heat and simmer for 30 minutes. Cool to room temperature.

Process the dough according to the directions. Roll out the dough and cut into two. Place half in a 9" (23 cm) spring form pan. Fill the pan with the cooled mixture, and sprinkle with the cheese. Cover with the remaining dough. Crimp edges to seal. Trim away any excess and use to decorate. Beat the egg and brush on the dough. Bake for 25-30 minutes in a preheated 450°F (230°C) oven, or until golden brown. Remove from the pan, slice and serve.

YIELDS one 9" (23 cm) pizza

Jamaican Jerk Chicken Pizza

Ingredients:

1 tbsp	15 ml	ground allspice
1 tbsp	15 ml	dried thyme
1 ½ tsp	8 ml	cayenne pepper
1 ½ tsp	8 ml	freshly ground black pepper
1 ½ tsp	8 ml	ground sage
¾ tsp	4 ml	ground nutmeg
¾ tsp	4 ml	ground cinnamon
2 tbsp	30 ml	salt
2 tbsp	30 ml	garlic powder
1 tbsp	15 ml	sugar
¼ cup	60 ml	olive oil
¼ cup	60 ml	soy sauce
¾ cup	180 ml	white vinegar
½ cup	125 ml	orange juice
3 tbsp	45 ml	lime juice
1	1	seeded and finely chopped Scotch bonnet pepper
1 cup	250 ml	chopped Bermuda onion
3	3	finely chopped scallions
4-6 oz	4-170 g	boneless, skinless chicken breasts
1 tsp	5 ml	cornstarch
2 tbsp	30 ml	water
1 lb	454 g	grocer purchased Gourmet Pizza Dough or 1 quantity of our recipe (see page 20)
1 cup	250 ml	sliced shiitake mushrooms
2 cups	500 ml	grated Colby cheese

Preparation:

In a large mixing bowl, combine the allspice, thyme, cayenne pepper, black pepper, sage, nutmeg, cinnamon, salt, garlic powder and sugar. With a wire whisk, slowly add the olive oil, soy sauce, vinegar, orange juice, and lime juice. Add the Scotch bonnet pepper, onion, and scallions and mix well.

Add the chicken breasts, cover and marinate for at least 3 hours.

Preheat an outdoor grill. Remove the breasts from the marinade and grill for 6 minutes on each side. While grilling, baste with the marinade. Cool and slice into bite size pieces. Heat the remaining marinade in a small saucepan, bring to a boil. Mix the cornstarch with the water and add to the marinade, simmer until thick.

Preheat the oven to 450°F (230°C).

Prepare the dough according to directions. Pan the dough into a 12" (30 cm) pizza pan. Spread the dough with the chicken, a small amount of thickened marinade, mushrooms and Colby cheese. Bake for 15 minutes or until golden brown.

Remove from the oven, slice and serve at once.

YIELDS one 12" (30 cm) pizza

Chef's Corner

Shiitake Mushrooms

Shiitake Mushrooms have a meaty flavor and are umbrella-shaped. They are great as a side dish or with stir-fried dishes. They are also known as Oak Mushrooms as they tend to grow on Oak trees. They are mainly grown in the Orient; however, they are widely available fresh throughout the world.

Basil & Pepper Focaccia

Ingredients:

2	2	crushed garlic cloves
2 tbsp	30 ml	red pepper olive oil
1 tbsp	15 ml	dried yeast
1 ½ cups	375 ml	warm water
1 tsp	5 ml	granulated sugar
3 ¾ cups	930 ml	unbleached all-purpose flour
1 ½ tsp	8 ml	salt
2	2	minced jalapeño peppers
¼ cup	60 ml	chopped basil leaves

TOPPING:

3 tbsp	45 ml	herbed olive oil
3	3	minced red casabel peppers
2 tbsp	30 ml	chopped basil leaves
1 tbsp	15 ml	coarse sea salt

FILLING:

3	3	each of red and yellow bell peppers
1	1	eggplant
¼ cup	60 ml	herbed olive oil
1 tsp	5 ml	each of sea salt and cracked black pepper
4	4	peeled, seeded and chopped tomatoes
2	2	thinly sliced red onions
¼ lb	120 g	sliced Provolone cheese
¼ lb	120 g	thinly sliced prosciutto
¼ lb	120 g	thinly sliced mortadella

Preparation:

Heat the garlic cloves in the olive oil over low heat until the garlic toasts. Remove and reserve the garlic and let the oil cool.

Stir the yeast into the water along with the sugar, let rise for 10 minutes. Add the cooled olive oil. Stir in the reserve toasted garlic, flour, salt, jalapeño and basil, blend well. Knead by hand for 6 to 8 minutes.

Place the dough into a lightly oiled bowl, cover and let rise until doubled. Place the dough into a 14" (33 cm) greased pizza pan. Stretch the dough to cover as much of the pan as possible. Cover and let it relax for 15 minutes. Dimple by pressing your finger throughout the dough. Stretch the dough once again to cover the pan. Allow to rise until it is light and airy about 50 minutes.

Preheat the oven to 400°F (200°C). Lightly dip your fingers into the herbed olive oil, dimple the top of the dough once again. Sprinkle with casabel peppers, basil and salt. Bake for 25 to 30 minutes until the dough is crispy on the edges. Cool briefly, then remove from the pan and cool on a rack.

While the focaccia cools, slice the red and yellow peppers along with the eggplant. Brush with the oil and sprinkle with salt and pepper. Grill on medium heat for 3-5 minutes.

Slice the focaccia in half and layer with the grilled vegetables, tomatoes, onions, cheese and meats.

YIELDS one 14" (33 cm) pizza

Chef's Corner

Andouille Sausage

Andouille Sausage is a highly seasoned pure pork sausage used extensively in Louisiana Cajun and Creole cookery. It originates from France. If you can't find Andouille, a hot Italian or a spicy Spanish Chorize may be substituted. It would be nearly impossible for anyone to list all the various sausages of the world. Germany alone has 1,500 varieties . Why not find those you enjoy, then search and find some more.

Potato and Chicken Calzone

Ingredients:

3 tbsp	45 ml	olive oil
8 oz	225 g	sliced boneless chicken breasts
1 tbsp	15 ml	chopped fresh rosemary
1 tsp	5 ml	minced garlic
		salt and pepper to taste
1 lb	454 g	grocer purchased Garlic and Parmesan Pizza Dough or 1 quantity of our recipe
1 cup	250 ml	Pizza Sauce (see page 14)
½ lb	225 g	par-boiled new potatoes, sliced into rounds
1 cup	250 ml	Ricotta cheese
1 cup	250 ml	grated smoked Gouda
⅓ cup	80 ml	grated Provolone
1	1	beaten egg

Preparation:

Heat the oil in a large skillet, add the chicken and sprinkle with the rosemary, garlic, salt and pepper.

Process the dough according to the directions.

Roll the dough into four rounds. Place two of the rounds into two 8" (20 cm) pizza pans.

Preheat the oven to 450°F (230°C).

Pour the Pizza Sauce evenly on each panned round. Cover the sauce with the chicken and potatoes.

Blend the cheeses together and place on the pizzas.

Place remaining rounds over the pizzas and crimp the edges to seal tightly. Brush with the egg. Poke with a fork to allow steam to escape.

Bake for 15-20 minutes or until golden brown.

YIELDS two 8" (20 cm) pizzas

Garlic Parmesan Dough

Ingredients:

2 tbsp	30 ml	dry active yeast
1 cup	250 ml	warm water
3½ cups	875 ml	unbleached flour (approximately)
4	4	minced garlic cloves
½ cup	125 ml	freshly grated Parmesan cheese
2	2	eggs, beaten
¼ cup	60 ml	olive oil

Preparation:

In a large mixing bowl, dissolve the yeast in the warm water. Rest 10 minutes or until foamy. Stir in 2 cups (500 ml) of flour along with the garlic, Parmesan, eggs and oil to form a smooth batter.

Gradually stir and knead in the remaining flour or enough to form a smooth ball. Place into a greased bowl. Cover and let rise 15 minutes. Divide the dough in half and roll into rounds on a lightly floured surface. Place onto lightly oiled pans. Let rise 15 minutes. With finger tips, press the dough from the centre out to cover the entire pan.

Dough is now ready for sauce and toppings.

YIELDS four 8" (20 cm) or two 12" (30 cm) pizzas

Buffalo Chicken Wing Pizza

Ingredients:

12 oz	345 g	boneless skinless chicken
¼ cup	60 ml	Frank Durkee's™ Louisiana Hot Sauce
¾ lb	340 g	grocer purchased Herb Dough or 1 quantity of our recipe
1 cup	250 ml	diced celery
1 cup	250 ml	Pizza Sauce (see page 14)
1 ½ cups	375 ml	crumbled blue cheese
1 ½ cups	375 ml	grated Brick cheese
1 cup	250 ml	grated Parmesan cheese
1 cup	250 ml	grated Provolone cheese

Preparation:

Dice the chicken and place into a mixing bowl. Pour the hot sauce over the chicken and marinate refrigerated for 1½ hours. Grill the chicken strips for 8-10 minutes.

Prepare the dough according to the directions.

Preheat the oven to 450°F (230°C).

Pan the dough according to instruction. Spoon the Pizza Sauce over the dough to ½" (1.5 cm) from the edge of the pan. Cover with the chicken, celery and sprinkle evenly with the cheeses.

Bake for 15 minutes or until the crust is golden. Remove from the pan, slice and serve.

YIELDS two 8" (20 cm) or one 12" (30 cm) pizzas

Herb Dough

Ingredients:

2 tbsp	30 ml	dry active yeast (2 envelopes)
1 ½ cups	375 ml	warm water
4 cups	1 L	all-purpose flour (approximately)
1 tsp	5 ml	salt
½ tsp	3 ml	each of dried basil, thyme, oregano, garlic powder, onion powder, chervil and black cracked pepper
¼ cup	60 ml	olive oil

Preparation:

In a large mixing bowl, dissolve the yeast in the warm water. Rest 10 minutes or until foamy.

Stir in 2 cups (500 ml) of flour along with the salt and seasonings. Stir to a smooth batter. Stir in the oil. Add 1 cup (250 ml) of flour, stirring into a ball. Add enough flour to form a smooth dough. Dough should not be sticky.

Knead the dough for 5 minutes, and allow to rise 15 minutes. Divide in half. Roll out into 11" (28 cm) circles. Let rise an additional 15 minutes. Place dough onto 12" (30 cm) lightly oiled pizza pans. With your finger tips, press dough from the centre to the edges until the pan is completely covered by dough.

Dough is now ready for sauce and toppings.

YIELDS four 8" (20 cm) or two 12" (30 cm) pizzas

Creme de Menthe Kahlua Pizza

Ingredients:

¼ cup	60 ml	butter
1 cup	250 ml	brown sugar - packed
1	1	egg
¼ cup	60 ml	Kahlua liqueur
¼ cup	60 ml	white Creme de Menthe liqueur
1½ cups	375 ml	flour
½ tsp	3 ml	baking powder
½ tsp	3 ml	baking soda
1 cup	250 ml	semi-sweet chocolate chips
2 tbsp	30 ml	green Creme de Menthe liqueur
1 cup	250 ml	confectioners' sugar

Preparation:

Cream the butter, sugar and egg, beating well. Whip in the Kahlua and White Creme de Menthe. Sift the flour, baking powder and baking soda together. Stir into the creamed mixture, fold in the chocolate chips. Pour batter into a buttered 12" (30 cm) pizza pan. Bake in a preheated 350°F (180°C) oven for 20-25 minutes.

Blend the Green Creme de Menthe and confectioners' sugar. Drizzle over the pizza. Cool and cut into slices.

YIELDS one 12" (30 cm) pizza.

Cookies and Cream Pizza

Ingredients:

1 lb	454 g	grocer purchased Sweet Dough or 1 quantity of our recipe
1	1	envelope of unflavored gelatin
¼ cup	60 ml	cold water
8 oz	225 g	cream cheese softened
½ cup	125 ml	granulated sugar
¼ cup	180 ml	milk
1 tsp	5 ml	vanilla extract
1 cup	250 ml	whipping cream, whipped
¼ cup	60 ml	raspberry preserves
1¼ cups	310 ml	chocolate cream-filled cookies, coarsely chopped

Preparation:

Preheat the oven to 400°F (200°C).

Prepare the dough according to directions. Roll out and line the bottom and sides of a 10" (30 cm) springform pan. Cover the dough with tin foil. Bake in the oven for 15 minutes or until golden brown. Cool to room temperature.

Soften the gelatin in the water; stir over low heat until dissolved. Combine the cream cheese, sugar and vanilla in a mixing bowl, beat until well blended. Gradually add the gelatin mixture and milk, mixing until well blended.

Chill until mixture is thickened but not set. Fold in the whipped cream. Spread the crust with the preserves. Pour ⅔ of the filling onto the crust, chill until set. Top with the cookies and reserved cream cheese mixture. Chill until firm.

YIELDS one 10" (30 cm) pizza

Sweet Dough

Ingredients:

1 tsp	5 ml	granulated sugar
1 cup	250 ml	warm water
1 tbsp	15 ml	(envelope) of active dry yeast
2 tbsp	30 ml	butter, melted and cooled
3½ cups	875 ml	all purpose flour
⅛ tsp	pinch	salt
2	2	eggs, beaten
¼ cup	60 ml	sugar
1 tbsp	15 ml	vanilla
1 tbsp	15 ml	lemon peel
1 tsp	5 ml	cinnamon

Preparation:

In a large bowl, dissolve the sugar in the warm water. Sprinkle with the yeast and let stand 10 minutes or until foamy. Stir in the butter.

Stir in half the flour along with, salt, eggs, sugar, vanilla, lemon peel and cinnamon into the yeast mixture. Gradually stir in enough of the remaining flour to make a slightly sticky ball.

Knead the dough on a lightly floured surface until smooth and elastic, about 5 minutes.

Place the dough into a greased bowl and let rise for 15 minutes. Punch down the dough; cut in half. Roll out each piece of dough into an 11" (28 cm) circle. Allow to rise again 15 minutes.

Place on a greased 12" (30 cm) pizza pan. With your finger tips press the dough to fill half the pan working from the centre. Rest dough for 10 minutes. Press once again until dough covers pan completely.

Dough is now ready for sauce and toppings

YIELDS two 12" (30 cm) pizzas

Chocolate Mountain Pizza

Ingredients:

Crust:

¾ cup	180 ml	corn syrup
⅓ cup	80 ml	whipping cream
8 oz	225 g	semi-sweet chocolate chips
½ cup	125 ml	butter
½ cup	125 ml	vanilla sugar
2	2	eggs, beaten
½ tsp	3 ml	vanilla extract
¾ cup	180 ml	flour
½ tsp	3 ml	salt
½ cup	125 ml	chopped pecans

Filling:

1 tbsp	15 ml	unflavored gelatin
⅓ cup	80 ml	water
½ lb	225 g	softened cream cheese
3 oz	80 g	melted chocolate chips
½ cup	125 ml	sweetened condensed milk
1 tsp	5 ml	vanilla
½ cup	125 ml	whipping cream, whipped

Topping:

¼ tsp	1 ml	salt
1 tsp	5 ml	vanilla
3 tbsp	45 ml	butter

Preparation:

Crust:

Preheat the oven to 350°F (180°C). Grease and flour a 12" (30 cm) pizza pan.

In a 12 cup (3L) saucepan heat the corn syrup and cream together until a rapid boil is achieved. Boil for 3 minutes. Remove from the heat and add the chocolate chips, stirring until chocolate melts. Reserve ⅔ cup (170 ml).

Add the butter and sugar, stirring until incorporated. Stir in the eggs and vanilla. Slowly stir in the flour, salt and nuts. Pour batter into the pizza pan and bake for 20 minutes or until an inserted toothpick comes out clean. Cool to room temperature.

Filling:

Soften the gelatin in the water, then heat until gelatin has dissolved. Remove from the heat and cool.

Cream the cheese with the chocolate, milk and vanilla. Stir in the gelatin. Fold in the whipped cream. Pour onto the pizza and refrigerate for 4 hours.

Topping:

Stir the salt, vanilla and butter into the reserved chocolate syrup, slice and serve the pizza, pouring the sauce over as you serve.

YIELDS one 12" (30 cm) pizza.

Apple Sauce Pizza

Ingredients:

⅓ cup	80 ml	butter
1 cup	250 ml	brown sugar - packed
1	1	egg
½ cup	125 ml	applesauce
2 tsp	10 ml	apple juice concentrate
1¼ cups	310 ml	flour
1 tsp	5 ml	baking powder
½ tsp	3 ml	baking soda
½ tsp	3 ml	salt
½ cup	125 ml	raisins - seedless
½ cup	125 ml	walnut pieces

Preparation:

Heat the butter and sugar in a saucepan until sugar is dissolved. Whip in the egg, applesauce and juice. Sift the flour together with the baking powder, baking soda and salt. Stir in the apple sauce. Fold in the raisins and walnuts. Pour onto a greased 12" (30 cm) pizza pan.

Bake for 25 minutes in a preheated 350°F (180°C) oven. Remove from the oven and glaze with Apple Glaze. Cut into slices.

YIELDS one 12" (30 cm) pizza

Apple Glaze

Ingredients:

1½ cups	375 ml	confectioners' sugar
2 tbsp	30 ml	apple juice concentrate

Preparation:

Blend the ingredients until smooth and pour over pizza.

YIELDS one 12" (30 cm) pizza.

Chef's Corner

Apples

Ever since Johnny Appleseed planted those first few seeds, apples have been falling onto heads of people like Sir Isaac Newton. But it takes more than gravity to cook a good apple. It takes the knowledge of what a good cooking apple is. Try using any of the following. They are all excellent for baking, sauces, pies, or just good eating. Baldwin, Empire, Red and Golden Delicious, Granny Smith, Ida Red, Lodi, Macintosh, Mutsu, Russet, as well as many others. Choose fresh, unbruised, firm fruit for the best results. Whenever possible don't pare the apples. The skin contains the major share of its nutritional value.

7-UP Blueberry Pizza

Ingredients:

¾ cup	180 ml	granulated sugar
½ cup	125 ml	all-purpose flour
⅛ tsp	pinch	salt
3 tbsp	45 ml	melted butter
1½ tsp	8 ml	lemon zest
¼ cup	60 ml	lemon juice
3	3	beaten egg yolks
1 cup	250 ml	7-UP®
½ cup	125 ml	milk
3	3	egg whites
1 cup	250 ml	fresh blueberries

Topping:

4 cups	1 L	blueberries
¼ cup	60 ml	granulated sugar
2 tbsp	30 ml	lemon juice
6 tbsp	90 ml	cornstarch
½ cup	125 ml	apple juice

Preparation:

Preheat the oven to 350°F (180°C).

In a large mixing bowl combine the sugar, flour, and salt. Stir in the butter, lemon zest, and lemon juice.

In a small bowl combine the eggs, 7-UP® and milk; add to the flour mixture.

Beat the egg whites to stiff peaks. Gently fold egg whites into lemon batter, stir in the blueberries. Turn into an ungreased 8"x8"x2" (20 x 20 x 5 cm) baking pan. Place in a larger pan on the oven's rack. Pour hot water into the larger pan to a depth of 1" (2.5 cm). Bake in the oven for 35 to 40 minutes or until the top is golden and springs back when touched.

Cool to room temperature. Refrigerate for 2 hours.

Topping:

In a saucepan, add the blueberries, sugar and lemon juice. Mix the cornstarch with the apple juice, add to the blueberry sauce. Simmer over low heat until mixture thickens. Cool, and ladle over the pizza slices as it is served.

SERVES 6

Rocky Road Pizza

Ingredients:

Dough:

½ tsp	3 ml	baking soda
2 tsp	10 ml	baking powder
2½ cups	625 ml	fine white flour
1 cup	250 ml	white sugar
½ cup	125 ml	shortening
2	2	eggs, beaten
1 tsp	5 ml	vanilla extract

Filling:

½ cup	125 ml	chopped peanuts
6 oz	180 g	semi-sweet chocolate chips
1 cup	250 ml	miniature marshmallows

Toppings:

3 oz	80 g	butterscotch chips
¾ cup	180 ml	confectioners' sugar
¼ cup	60 ml	boiling water
1 cup	250 ml	whipping cream
1 tsp	5 ml	vanilla extract

Preparation:

Dough:

Sift the soda, baking powder and flour together. Cream the sugar and shortening together until light. Add one egg at a time until all have been incorporated. Stir in the vanilla. Add the flour gradually to blend. Place the dough onto wax paper and roll. Chill refrigerated for 1 hour.

Filling:

Preheat the oven to 350°F (180°C). Slice the chilled dough into ¼" (6 mm) thick slices. Arrange on the bottom of a lightly greased 12" (30 cm) pizza pan. Bake for 10-12 minutes or until golden brown. While the pizza is hot sprinkle with the peanuts, chocolate chips and marshmallows. Bake for an additional 3-5 minutes or until chocolate and marshmallows are melted.

Toppings:

In a double boiler melt the butterscotch chips. Stir in the sugar and water. Remove from the heat and cool.

Whip the cream and fold into the butterscotch. Add the vanilla. Pour sauce over the warm pizza as you serve it.

YIELDS one 12" (30 cm) pizza.

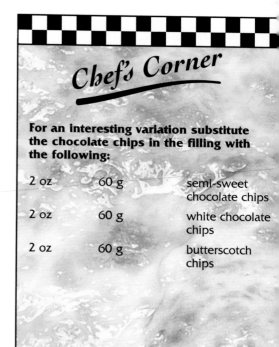

Chef's Corner

For an interesting variation substitute the chocolate chips in the filling with the following:

2 oz	60 g	semi-sweet chocolate chips
2 oz	60 g	white chocolate chips
2 oz	60 g	butterscotch chips

Peanut Butter Pizza

Ingredients:
Dough:

½ tsp	3 ml	baking soda
2 tsp	10 ml	baking powder
2½ cups	625 ml	fine white flour
1 cup	250 ml	white sugar
½ cup	125 ml	shortening
2	2	eggs, beaten
½ tsp	3 ml	vanilla extract
1 cup	250 ml	buttermilk

Filling:

½ cup	125 ml	peanut butter
3 oz	80 g	cream cheese, softened
3 tbsp	45 ml	vanilla sugar*
⅛ tsp	pinch	salt
3 tbsp	45 ml	soft butter
2 tbsp	30 ml	light cream
1 tbsp	15 ml	vanilla
¼ cup	60 ml	raspberry preserves
1-2 tbsp	15-30 ml	water
3	3	sliced bananas
½ cup	125 ml	chopped peanuts

Topping:

1 lb	454 g	fresh raspberries
2 tbsp	30 ml	lemon juice
3 tbsp	45 ml	sugar
3 oz	80 g	grated semi-sweet chocolate
1 tbsp	15 ml	butter

Preparation:
Dough:

Sift the soda, powder and flour together. Cream the sugar and shortening together until light. Add one egg at a time until all have been incorporated. Stir in the vanilla. Alternating thirds, stir in the flour and buttermilk. Place dough onto wax paper and roll, chill refrigerated for 1 hour.

Preheat the oven to 375°F (190°C). Slice the chilled dough into ¼" (6 mm) thick slices. Arrange on the bottom of a lightly greased 12" (30 cm) pizza pan. Bake for 10-12 minutes or until golden brown, cool to room temperature.

Filling:

In a food processor with a chilled cutting blade and bowl, cream the peanut butter and cream cheese together. Add the vanilla sugar, salt, butter and vanilla. Whip until very light.

Mix enough water with the raspberry preserves so that it will spread easily. Spread on the bottom of the crust. Cover with the creamed mixture. Chill refrigerated for 1-2 hours. Arrange the bananas on top and sprinkle with chopped peanuts.

Topping:

While pizza chills, purée the raspberries in a food processor. Press through a sieve (to remove seeds) into a small saucepan.

Add the lemon juice and sugar, bring to a boil. Reduce the heat and simmer to 1 cup (250 ml). Stir in the chocolate. Remove from the heat and whip in the butter. Cool to room temperature. Pour over pizza when serving.

YIELDS one 12" (30 cm) pizza.

* If you can't find vanilla sugar in your store, you may make it by placing 1-2 vanilla beans into 2 cups (500 ml) of white sugar. Place in an air tight container and store for two weeks in a cool dark place.

Buttertart Pizza

Ingredients:

½ cup	125 ml	butter
1 cup	250 ml	flour
1¾ cups	430 ml	brown sugar
2	2	eggs-beaten
½ cup	125 ml	oatmeal
¼ tsp	1 ml	salt
½ tsp	3 ml	baking powder
1 tsp	5 ml	vanilla
½ cup	125 ml	pecans - broken
½ cup	125 ml	raisins

Preparation:

Cut the butter with the flour and 2 tbsp (30 ml) of sugar. Press onto a buttered 12" (30 cm) pizza pan. Bake in a preheated 350°F (180°C) oven for 15 minutes.

Beat the eggs with the remaining sugar. Fold in the oatmeal, salt and baking powder. Blend well. Stir in the vanilla, nuts and raisins.

Pour into shell and return to the oven and bake for an additional 20 minutes. Cool before cutting into slices.

YIELDS one 12" (30 cm) pizza.

Banana Split Pizza

Ingredients:

Brownie:

½ cup	125 ml	butter
½ cup	125 ml	oil
1 cup	250 ml	water
4 tbsp	60 ml	unsweetened cocoa
2 cups	500 ml	all purpose flour
2 cups	500 ml	granulated sugar
2	2	eggs
1 tsp	5 ml	baking soda
½ cup	125 ml	buttermilk
1 tsp	5 ml	vanilla extract

Toppings:

8 oz	225 g	softened cream cheese
⅔ cup	170 ml	sweetened condensed milk
1 tsp	5 ml	vanilla extract
1 cup	250 ml	banana slices
20	20	Fresh large strawberries, cleaned & hulled
10 oz	280 g	chocolate chips
1 tbsp	15 ml	butter

Preparation:

Preheat the oven to 350°F (180°C). Grease and flour a 9" x 13" baking pan.

Mix butter, oil, water and cocoa together in a small saucepan. Bring to a boil. Add to the flour and sugar and beat until smooth.

Add the eggs, baking soda, buttermilk and vanilla. Mix well. Pour onto the prepared baking pan. Bake for 20 minutes. Cool to room temperature.

Beat the cream cheese until fluffy. Slowly add the milk beating until very light. Stir in the juice and vanilla. Chill thoroughly until thick. Spoon over the crust and garnish with the bananas and strawberries.

Melt the chocolate and butter in a double boiler and drizzle over the pizza. Chill for 45 minutes. Serve.

YIELDS 24 slices

Chef's Corner

To prevent bananas or any other fruit from oxidizing (turning brown) sprinkle the sliced fruit with a small amount of lemon juice or sugar water.

Honolulu Pizza

Ingredients:

Crust:

1 1/2 cups	375 ml	sugar
4	4	eggs - beaten
1/2 cup	125 ml	melted butter
1 1/2 cups	375 ml	flour
1/2 cup	125 ml	shredded coconut
3/4 cup	180 ml	macadamia nuts - pieces
1/2 tsp	3 ml	baking soda
1/2 tsp	3 ml	salt
2 cups	500 ml	crushed pineapple, drained

Topping:

1 cup	250 ml	whipping cream
1/4 cup	60 ml	confectioners' sugar
2 1/2 cups	625 ml	crushed pineapple with juice
3 oz	80 g	pineapple or vanilla instant pudding

Preparation:

Crust:

In a mixing bowl beat the sugar into the eggs. Whip the butter. Fold in the remaining ingredients. Pour onto a greased 12" (30 cm) pizza pan.

Bake in a preheated 350°F (180°C) oven for 30-35 minutes. Cool completely.

Topping:

Whip the cream until it forms soft peaks. Whip in the confectioners' sugar. Whip the pineapple together with the pudding until set. Fold in the whipping cream. Spoon over cooled pizza shell. Slice and serve.

YIELDS one 12" (30 cm) pizza

Pasta

The exact origins of pasta are unknown. Every nation of the world holds some kind of "strips of paste" recipes in their cuisine. Pasta has made its mark in cuisine from as far back as the Chinese Ming Dynasty. It is thought that Marco Polo introduced "noodles" to Italy upon his return from far away Asiatic countries during his 13th century expedition to China.

Pasta, however, was known to Italy before then. Prince Theodric of the Teutonic tribe from the Vistual area, invaded Italy in approximately 405 A.D. and brought with him a type of noodle. Yet there is evidence that noodles existed even

earlier. Imperial Rome had a noodle very simila to the tagliatelle noodle (1" wide long noodles also called mafalda) that was known as laganu What is known is that upon the return of Marc Polo, the noodle became a popular staple of th Italian people.

From Italy the pasta noodle (tagliarini) spread throughout Europe, becoming the "nouilles" of France, the "fideos" of Spain, the "nudein" c Germany and the "noodle" in England.

Today pasta has taken the world into all new culinary expeditions and will never be satisfied

be limited to strictly tomato or cream based
auces again. Here, in The Original Pizza & Pasta
ookbook we have given an offering of unique
nd creative dishes that even Marco would never
ave dreamed possible. Such dishes as
Mediterranean Radiatore, or Seafood Linguine with
oasted Red Pepper Pesto would have thrilled the
ncient explorer, as they will your guests.

hroughout this book, we have given appetizers
oups, salads, entrées and even dessert pastas.
n entire five course gourmet meal with the
cus on pasta can be created from these pasta
esentations alone.

You may only dream of such things as chocolate
pasta, but it is within these pages. Offer your
guest the Expresso Cannoli with the Coffee
Chocolate Sauce. Or, better yet, use any one of
our 15 different pasta doughs and create your
own special pasta dishes, based upon your
distinct character. One thing you may be
absolutely certain of, the final results will offer a
unique eating experience.

Mediterranean Radiatore

Ingredients:

12 oz	345 g	radiatore
1 cup	250 ml	marinated artichoke hearts, drained
12 oz	345 g	boneless, skinless chicken breasts
2 tbsp	30 ml	olive oil
2 tbsp	30 ml	all-purpose flour
½ cup	125 ml	heavy cream
1½ cups	375 ml	stewed tomatoes
2 tbsp	30 ml	chopped fresh parsley
2 tsp	10 ml	chopped fresh basil
1 tsp	5 ml	Dijon mustard with seeds
¼ lb	115 g	julienne sliced prosciutto
3 tbsp	45 ml	ripe black olives, sliced
		salt and freshly ground pepper to taste
¼ cup	60 ml	grated Romano cheese

Preparation:

Prepare the pasta according to package directions. While the pasta is cooking, squeeze as much water from the artichoke hearts as possible and cut each piece in half lengthwise.

Cut the chicken into 1" (2.5 cm) cubes

Heat the oil in a large skillet over medium heat. Add the chicken and artichoke hearts. Sauté, stirring frequently, until the chicken is golden brown, about 6 minutes.

Sprinkle the chicken with the flour, reduce heat and cook for 2 minutes. Add the cream and simmer until the sauce is thick. Add the tomatoes, parsley, basil and mustard. Bring to a boil, reduce heat and simmer until the sauce is reduce to half its volume. Stir in the prosciutto.

Drain the pasta and return it to it's pot. Pour the sauce over the pasta, add the olives. Check the seasoning and adjust with salt and pepper if required.

Serve in hot bowls and sprinkle with the cheese.

SERVES 4

SAUCE:

Ingredients:

1 tbsp	15 ml	unsalted butter
3 oz	80 g	sliced mushroom
½ lb	225 g	cooked, smoked chicken meat, diced
6	6	coarsely chopped sun-dried tomatoes
3 cups	750 ml	Mornay Sauce (see page 12)

Preparation:

Heat the butter in a saucepan. Sauté the mushrooms in the butter. Add the chicken, tomatoes and Mornay Sauce and reduce to a simmer. Simmer for 10 minutes.

SERVES 6

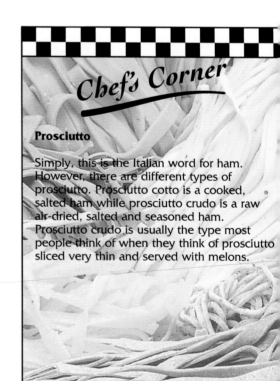

Chef's Corner

Prosciutto

Simply, this is the Italian word for ham. However, there are different types of prosciutto. Prosciutto cotto is a cooked, salted ham while prosciutto crudo is a raw air-dried, salted and seasoned ham. Prosciutto crudo is usually the type most people think of when they think of prosciutto sliced very thin and served with melons.

Seafood Linguine
with Roasted Red Pepper Pesto

Ingredients:

1 lb	454 g	grocer purchased pasta or 1 quantity of our Basic Pasta Dough recipe (see page 78)
½ lb	225 g	cleaned and sliced squid tubes
½ lb	225 g	peeled & de-veined prawns
¼ tsp	1 ml	garlic powder
¼ tsp	1 ml	onion powder
1 tsp	5 ml	oregano leaves
½ tsp	3 ml	cracked black pepper
½ tsp	3 ml	salt
1	1	garlic clove
1 cup	250 ml	diced roasted red bell peppers
¼ cup	60 ml	olive oil
1 tbsp	15 ml	basil leaves
3 tbsp	45 ml	parsley
3 oz	80 g	freshly grated Romano cheese
2 tbsp	30 ml	pine nuts
3 tbsp	45 ml	butter

Preparation:

Process the pasta as directed. Cut into linguine.

Place the squid and prawns in a large mixing bowl, sprinkle with the seasonings.

In a food processor or blender, purée the garlic and bell peppers in the oil. Add the basil, parsley, Romano cheese and pine nuts. Continue to process into a purée.

Heat the butter in a large skillet and add the seafood, sauté for 5-6 minutes.

While the seafood cooks, boil the linguine in a kettle of boiling salted water al dente. Drain the linguine and toss with the pesto. Place on serving plates. Top with the seafood and serve.

SERVES 6

Zucchini Lasagna
with Five Cheeses

Ingredients:

Sauce:

3 tbsp	45 ml	olive oil
1	1	minced garlic clove
1	1	finely diced medium onion
2	2	finely diced celery stalks
2	2	finely diced small zucchini
4 oz	120 g	sliced mushrooms
1 tsp	5 ml	each of salt, basil leaves
½ tsp	3 ml	each of thyme leaves, oregano leaves, paprika, pepper
¼ tsp	1 ml	cayenne pepper
3 lbs	1.5 kg	peeled, seeded and chopped tomatoes

Pasta:

2 lbs	900 g	grocer purchased Pasta Verde Dough or 1 quantity of our recipe (see page 110)
1 cup	250 ml	Ricotta cheese
1 cup	250 ml	grated Cheddar cheese
1 cup	250 ml	grated Monterey Jack cheese
¼ cup	60 ml	grated Romano cheese
¼ cup	60 ml	grated Parmesan cheese
3 tbsp	45 ml	chopped chives
1 tsp	5 ml	basil leaves
½ tsp	3 ml	each of cracked black pepper, salt
2	2	eggs

Preparation:

Sauce:

In a large saucepan, heat the oil. Add the garlic, onion, celery, zucchini and mushrooms. Sauté until tender.

Add the seasonings and tomatoes. Simmer over low heat for 3 hours or until desired thickness is achieved.

Pasta:

Process pasta as directed. Cut into lasagna noodles. Cook in 8 cups (2L) of boiling salted water, drain and rinse under cold water.

In a mixing bowl, blend the cheeses with the seasonings and eggs.

Spoon mixture onto noodles and roll in a jelly roll fashion.

Place in a baking dish. Cover with the sauce. Bake in a 375°F (190°C) preheated oven for 30 minutes, covered. Remove cover and continue to bake for an additional 15 minutes. Serve.

SERVES 6

Chef's Corner

Always preheat your oven before baking, broiling or roasting. This will ensure your cooking times are accurate.

66

Latin Penne Tortilla Bowl

Ingredients:

1 lb	454 g	penne noodles
1 tbsp	15 ml	vegetable oil
1	1	chopped medium onion
1	1	minced garlic clove
1	1	seeded and minced jalapeño
½ lb	225 g	diced chorizo sausage
1 tsp	5 ml	salt
½ tsp	3 ml	pepper
1 tsp	5 ml	Worcestershire sauce
3 tbsp	45 ml	chili powder
1 tsp	5 ml	cumin
1 tsp	5 ml	dried oregano
3 cups	750 ml	stewed tomatoes
1 lb	454 g	cooked boneless, skinless chicken breast, julienned
6	6	tortilla shell bowls
1 cup	250 ml	grated Monterey Jack cheese
1 cup	250 ml	tomato salsa sauce
½ cup	125 ml	guacamole sauce
½ cup	125 ml	sour cream
¼ cup	60 ml	ripe olives

Preparation:

Preheat the oven to broil.

Prepare the pasta according to package directions.

While the pasta is cooking, heat the oil in a medium saucepan over medium heat. Add the onion, garlic, jalapeño and sausage, sauté until the sausage is cooked through. Add the salt, pepper, Worcestershire, chili powder, cumin, oregano and tomatoes.

Stir in the chicken. Simmer until slightly thickened, about 15 minutes. Mix in the pasta and continue to simmer for 5 minutes.

Spoon the mixture into the tortilla shells and place onto a baking sheet. Sprinkle with the cheese and broil in the oven to golden brown.

Place on serving plates and top with salsa, guacamole, sour cream and olives.

SERVES 6

New Orleans Stuffed Shells

Ingredients:

24	24	jumbo shells
2 tsp	10 ml	vegetable oil
1	1	chopped medium onion
½ lb	225 g	lean ground beef
½ lb	225 g	andouille sausage
1 tsp	5 ml	chili powder
1- 4oz	1-115 g	can of chopped green chilies, drained
1 cup	250 ml	Ricotta cheese
1 cup	250 ml	grated Monterey Jack cheese
3½ cups	875 ml	Creole Sauce

Preparation:

Prepare pasta according to package directions, drain. Reserve in cold water.

In a medium saucepan heat the oil, add the onion, ground beef and sausage meat, cook over medium heat until browned. Remove from the heat and drain excess fat. Add the chili powder, chopped green chilies, Ricotta, ½ cup (125 ml) grated Monterey Jack cheese and ½ of the Creole Sauce mixture to the meat mixture.

Preheat the oven to 350°F (180°C).

Pour half of the remaining Creole Sauce on the bottom of a 13 x 9 x 2-inch baking dish. Fill each cooked shell with 2 tablespoons of meat\cheese mixture and place the shells in the baking dish.

Pour the remaining Creole Sauce over top of the shells. Cover with aluminum foil and bake for 20 to 30 minutes. Uncover, add remaining ½ cup (125 ml) of Monterey Jack cheese and bake, uncovered, an additional 5 minutes or until cheese melts. Serve immediately.

SERVES 6

Creole Sauce

Ingredients:

3 tbsp	45 ml	safflower oil
3	3	finely diced onions
2	2	finely diced green bell peppers
3	3	finely diced celery stalks
20	20	peeled, seeded and chopped tomatoes
2 tsp	10 ml	salt
2 tsp	10 ml	paprika
1 tsp	5 ml	garlic powder
1 tsp	5 ml	onion powder
1 tsp	5 ml	cayenne pepper
½ tsp	3 ml	white pepper
½ tsp	3 ml	black pepper
1 tsp	5 ml	dried basil leaves
½ tsp	3 ml	dried oregano leaves
½ tsp	3 ml	dried thyme leaves
6	6	diced green onions
1	1	bunch chopped parsley

Preparation:

Heat the oil in a large saucepan. Sauté the onions, green peppers and celery until tender. Add the tomatoes and seasonings, simmering gently until desired thickness has been achieved (about 4 hours).

Add the green onions and parsley. Simmer 15 minutes longer. Sauce is ready for use.

YIELDS 4-6 cups (1-1.5 L)

Lobster Mafalda

Ingredients:

1½ lbs	675 g	grocer purchased Basic Pasta Dough or 1 quantity of our recipe (see page 78), cut into 1" wide strips
3 tbsp	45 ml	unsalted butter
4 oz	120 g	sliced mushrooms
3 tbsp	45 ml	all purpose flour
1½ cups	375 ml	chicken stock (see page 146)
½ cup	125 ml	half & half cream
1 lb	454 g	cooked diced lobster meat
½ cup	125 ml	freshly grated Parmesan cheese
½ cup	125 ml	freshly grated Romano cheese

Preparation:

Cook the noodles (mafalda) in a large kettle of salted boiling water. Drain. Rinse under cold water and reserve.

Heat the butter in a sauce pan. Sauté the mushrooms in the butter. Add the flour. Cook for 2 minutes over low heat. Add the chicken stock and cream. Simmer until thickened.

Add the lobster and half the cheese.

Place the noodles in a greased casserole dish. Pour the sauce over the noodles. Sprinkle with remaining cheese. Bake in a preheated 325°F (160°C) oven for 30 minutes or until lightly browned. Serve at once.

SERVES 6

Blackened Shrimp with
Black Pepper Linguini

Ingredients:

Do this outside on your gas barbecue, it's very smoky.

¾ lb	340 g	grocer purchased Cracked Black Pepper Pasta Dough or 1 quantity of our recipe
1 lb	454 g	peeled and de-veined large shrimp
1 tbsp	15 ml	each of salt, chili powder
1 tsp	5 ml	each of thyme leaves, oregano leaves, basil, black pepper, paprika, chervil
½ tsp	3 ml	each of white pepper, cayenne pepper
¼ cup	60 ml	safflower oil
⅓ cup	80 ml	butter
3	3	minced garlic cloves
3 tbsp	45 ml	lemon juice
½ cup	125 ml	grated Parmesan cheese
2 tbsp	30 ml	fresh chopped parsley

Preparation:

Prepare pasta as per instructions. Cut into linguini.

Rinse the shrimp under cold water. Drain. Blend the seasonings together. Dust the shrimp in the seasonings. Heat the oil to very hot just before the smoking point. Fry the shrimp in the hot oil for 3 minutes. Transfer to a platter and reserve.

Cook the pasta in a large kettle of salted boiling water. While the pasta cooks, heat the butter in a skillet. Add the garlic and lemon juice. Cook for 3 minutes. Drain pasta and pour the butter over. Sprinkle with cheese and toss to coat.

Place on serving plates and top with shrimp. Sprinkle with parsley. Serve.

SERVES 4.

Cracked Black Pepper Pasta
Ingredients:

1 tbsp	15 ml	fresh cracked black pepper
3	3	eggs, beaten
2 cups	500 ml	semolina flour
		ice water, only if required

Preparation:

In a mixing bowl blend the pepper in the eggs. Slowly add the flour. Knead into a soft ball (add small amounts of ice water if required).

Knead the dough for 15 minutes and allow to rest for an additional 15 minutes. Roll out the dough. Lightly dust with flour, fold in three and roll out again. Repeat 6 to 8 times.

Now pass the dough through the pasta machine setting the rollers gradually down until you reach the desired thickness. The result should be a smooth sheet of dough ready to process as you require.

SERVES 4

Chef's Corner

Chili Powder

Chili Powder is a blend of differing capsicum peppers (chilies), with different degrees of hotness.

Pork Soong

Ingredients:

¾ lb	345 g	pork tenderloin
3 tbsp	45 ml	peanut oil
½ lb	225 g	shrimp
¾ cup	180 ml	bamboo shoots
½ cup	125 ml	thinly sliced water chestnuts
1 cup	250 ml	peas
¾ cup	180 ml	chicken broth (see page 146)
3 tbsp	45 ml	sherry
3 tbsp	45 ml	light soy sauce
1 tbsp	15 ml	honey
2 tsp	10 ml	cornstarch
¾ lb	340 g	grocer purchased Egg Pasta Dough or 1 quantity of our recipe (see page 122)

Preparation:

Dice the pork into ¾" cubes.

Heat the oil in a wok or large skillet. Sauté the pork with the shrimp until cooked through. Add the bamboo, water chestnuts and peas. Stir fry for 2 minutes.

Blend the broth, sherry, soy sauce, honey and cornstarch together. Add to stir fry and simmer until thickened.

While the stir fry is cooking, boil 2 quarts (2 L) of salted water in a kettle. Cook the noodles for 2-3 minutes. Drain. Transfer to a serving dish.

Pour stir fry over noodles. Serve.

SERVES 6

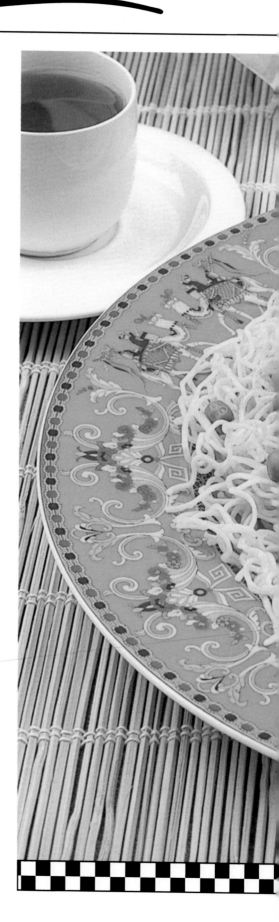

77

Spaghetti Al Granseola

Ingredients:

1 lb	454 g	grocer purchased Basic Pasta Dough or 1 quantity of our recipe
2 tbsp	30 ml	olive oil
2	2	minced garlic cloves
1	1	diced small onion
1 tsp	5 ml	crushed red chilies
1 tbsp	5 ml	minced fresh basil
2 cups	500 ml	peeled, seeded and diced tomatoes
1 lb	454 g	Dungeness crab meat
2 tbsp	30 ml	butter
2 tbsp	30 ml	all-purpose flour
1 cup	250 ml	milk
½ tsp	3 ml	salt
½ tsp	3 ml	white pepper
⅛ tsp	pinch	nutmeg
¼ cup	60 ml	grated hard Cacciocavallo cheese

Preparation:

Process the pasta as directed and cut into spaghetti noodles.

In a saucepan heat the oil, add the garlic and onion, sauté until tender. Add the chilies, basil and tomatoes, reduce the heat and simmer for 20 minutes. Stir in the crab meat.

In a second saucepan heat the butter, add the flour and cook over low heat for 2 minutes. Stir in the milk and seasonings, simmer until thick. Stir the cream sauce into the tomato sauce and blend.

While sauces are simmering cook the pasta al dente in 8 cups (2 L) of boiling salted water. Drain, place on serving plates, smother with sauce and sprinkle with the cheese.

SERVES 6

Basic Pasta Dough

Ingredients:

4 cups	1 L	semolina flour
½ tsp	3 ml	salt
4	4	eggs
1 tbsp	15 ml	oil
⅓ cup	80 ml	ice cold water

Preparation:

Sift the flour and salt together. Place into a mixing bowl. Slowly blend in the eggs, one at a time. Add the oil and the water slowly until a smooth soft dough is formed.

Knead the dough for 15 minutes and allow to sit for an additional 15 minutes. Roll out the dough. Lightly dust with flour, fold in three and roll out again.* Repeat 6 to 8 times.

Now pass the dough through a pasta machine setting the rollers gradually down until you reach the desired thickness. The result should be a smooth sheet of dough ready to process as you require.

Pass through a pasta machine, or cut by hand to desired size. If processed by hand, simply roll the dough and cut into thin strips for noodles (fettucini) or into wider strips for lasagna, cannelloni, ravioli, etc.

* Use only enough flour to prevent sticking while rolling.

SERVES 6

Scallop & Shrimp Double Wong

Ingredients:

¾ lb	340 g	grocer purchased Egg Pasta Dough or 1 quantity of our recipe (see page 122)
4 tbsp	60 ml	peanut oil
½ lb	225 g	peeled and de-veined shrimp
½ lb	225 g	bay scallops
3 oz	80 g	thinly sliced mushrooms
½ cup	125 ml	finely diced onion
½ cup	125 ml	finely diced celery
1 tbsp	15 ml	light soy sauce
2 tbsp	30 ml	sherry

Preparation:

In a kettle cook the noodles. Drain and reserve.

In a wok or large skillet heat 2 tbsp (30 ml) of oil. Quickly cook the shrimp, scallops and vegetables. Add the remaining oil. Cook for 1 additional minute. Add the noodles and fry quickly on one side. Turn the noodles over and fry for 1 additional minute. Add the soy sauce and sherry, continue to fry for 1 minute. Transfer to a serving plate. Serve at once.

SERVES 6

Mushroom Thyme Chicken Linguine

Ingredients:

1 lb	454 g	grocer purchased Basic Pasta Dough or 1 quantity of our recipe (see page 78)
2 tbsp	30 ml	olive oil
1	1	chopped onion
1	1	minced garlic clove
1 lb	454 g	sliced mushrooms
1 tbsp	15 ml	chopped fresh thyme
¼ tsp	1 ml	nutmeg
2 tbsp	30 ml	all-purpose flour
2 cups	500 ml	light cream
¼ lb	120 g	cooked diced chicken
½ cup	125 ml	chopped fresh parsley
¾ tsp	4 ml	salt
½ tsp	3 ml	cracked pepper

Preparation:

Process the pasta as directed and cut in linguine noodles.

In a large skillet, heat the oil over medium heat; cook the onion and garlic until translucent. Add the mushrooms, thyme and nutmeg; continue cooking uncovered for 5 minutes. Sprinkle with flour; cook, stirring, for 1 minute. Gradually whisk in the cream; cook, stirring, until thick.

Cook the linguine in 8 cups (2 L) of boiling salted water until al dente, drain.

Toss the linguine with the sauce, chicken, ⅓ cup (80 ml) of the parsley, salt and pepper. Transfer to a platter; garnish with remaining parsley.

SERVES 6

Beef Broth or Stock

Ingredients:

2 lbs	1 kg	meaty beef bones
¼ cup	60 ml	olive oil
10 cups	2.5 L	cold water
2	2	coarsely chopped celery stalks
2	2	coarsely chopped large carrots
1	1	coarsely chopped onion
1	1	bouquet garni** (see page 146)
1 tsp	3 ml	salt

Preparation:

Place the bones in a roaster and cover with oil. Bake in a preheated 350°F (180°C) oven for 1 hour or until the bones are well-browned. Transfer to a large kettle or Dutch oven.

Add the water and remaining ingredients. Bring to a simmer. Simmer uncovered for 3-4 hours, skimming any impurities that may rise to the top.

Remove the meat (reserve and use as required). Discard bones, bouquet garni and vegetables. Strain through a cheesecloth or fine sieve.

Chill the stock and remove any fat from the surface.

Allow stock to chill for 24 hours before using. Use for soups and sauces or as required.

YIELDS 4-6 cups (1-1.5 L)

Pork & Shrimp Vermicelli

Ingredients:

¾ lb	345 g	vermicelli
3 tbsp	45 ml	peanut oil *
2 tsp	10 ml	minced ginger root
1	1	minced garlic clove
1 lb	454 g	pork, shredded
½ lb	225 g	shrimp
4 oz	120 g	sliced mushrooms
3 tbsp	45 ml	oyster sauce
½ tsp	3 ml	cayenne pepper
2 tbsp	30 ml	soy sauce
1 tbsp	15 ml	sherry
2 tsp	10 ml	cornstarch

Preparation:

In a large kettle of boiling salted water, cook the noodles. Drain and reserve.

In a wok, heat the oil. Quickly fry the ginger and garlic. Add the pork, shrimp and mushrooms. Cook thoroughly. Add the noodles. Fry 1 minute per side.

Blend the oyster sauce, cayenne, soy sauce, sherry and cornstarch. Pour over vermicelli noodles. Fry 1-2 additional minutes. Serve at once.

SERVES 6

* Use safflower oil if you desire

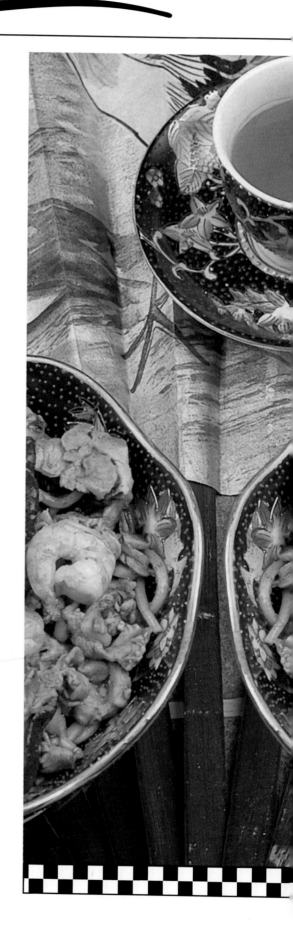

Spaghetti Chef K Style

Ingredients:

1 lb	454 g	grocer purchased Basic Pasta Dough our 1 quantity of our recipe, (see page 78)
3 tbsp	45 ml	olive oil
10 oz	280 g	extra lean ground beef
4 oz	120 g	thin sliced prosciutto
4 oz	120 g	ground hot Italian sausage meat
1	1	finely diced Spanish onion
2	2	finely diced green bell peppers
2	2	finely diced celery stalks
2	2	minced garlic cloves
½ cup	125 ml	chopped fresh parsley
¼ cup	60 ml	tomato paste
2 cups	500 ml	Marinara Sauce (see page 180)
1 ½ cups	375 ml	red wine
1 tsp	5 ml	salt
½ tsp	3 ml	oregano
½ tsp	3 ml	thyme
½ tsp	3 ml	basil
½ tsp	3 ml	black pepper
1	1	bay leaf
1 tsp	5 ml	Worcestershire sauce
4 cups	1 L	salted water
⅓ cup	80 ml	grated Parmesan cheese

Preparation:

Process the pasta as directed and cut into spaghetti.

In a large skillet heat the oil. Fry the meats thoroughly. Drain excess oil. Add the vegetables and continue to cook until the vegetables are tender.

Add the parsley, tomato paste, Marinara Sauce, wine, seasonings and Worcestershire Reduce the heat and simmer for 30 minutes Discard the bay leaf.

In a large kettle of boiling salted water, cook the spaghetti until al denté. Drain and place on serving plates. Spoon the sauce over and sprinkle with the Parmesan cheese. Serve at once.

SERVES 4

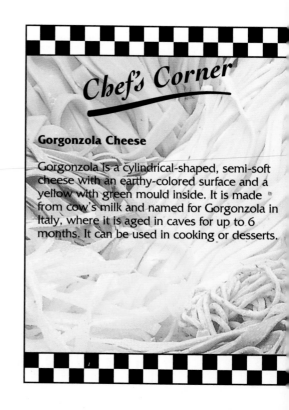

Gorgonzola Cheese

Gorgonzola is a cylindrical-shaped, semi-soft cheese with an earthy-colored surface and a yellow with green mould inside. It is made from cow's milk and named for Gorgonzola in Italy, where it is aged in caves for up to 6 months. It can be used in cooking or desserts.

Pappardelle Alla Pamela

Ingredients:

4 tbsp	60 ml	butter
1 cup	250 ml	sliced porcini mushrooms
4 tbsp	60 ml	all-purpose flour
2 cups	500 ml	milk
½ tsp	3 ml	salt
½ tsp	3 ml	white pepper
⅛ tsp	pinch	nutmeg
3 oz	90 g	sliced prosciutto
½ cup	125 ml	shelled peas
¼ cup	60 ml	grated Parmesan cheese
1 lb	454 g	black pappardelle noodles *

Preparation:

Melt the butter in a saucepan. Sauté the mushrooms. Add the flour and stir into a paste (roux). Cook for 2 minutes over low heat.

Add the milk and stir. Simmer until thickened. Add the seasonings and simmer for 2 additional minutes. Stir in the prosciutto, peas and cheese, simmer for an additional 5 minutes.

While sauce simmers cook the pappardelle in 8 cups (2 L) of boiling salted water until al dente. Drain and put the noodles on a serving plate and smother with sauce. Serve.

SERVES 6

* Black colored noodles are made from the ink produced from a squid.

88

Trumpetti Campanola

Ingredients:

2	2	yellow bell peppers
1 lb	454 g	hot Italian sausage meat
2 tbsp	30 ml	olive oil
1	1	large Spanish onion
1 cup	250 ml	quartered marinated artichokes
3 oz	90 g	sliced porcini mushrooms
2 cups	500 ml	peeled, seeded and diced tomatoes
2 tbsp	30 ml	butter
2 tbsp	30 ml	all-purpose flour
1 cup	250 ml	milk
¼ tsp	1 ml	salt
¼ tsp	1 ml	white pepper
⅛ tsp	pinch	nutmeg
1 lb	454 g	Trumpet shaped pasta*

Preparation:

Preheat the oven to 400°F (200°C) and roast the peppers for 20 minutes. Remove from the oven and peel away the skin. Remove the core, seeds and membranes, dice fine.

In a saucepan brown the sausage meat, drain excess fat. Add the oil and sauté the onion, artichokes and mushrooms until tender. Add the diced yellow peppers and tomatoes. Reduce heat and simmer for 30 minutes.

Melt the butter in a second sauce pan. Add the flour and stir into a paste (roux) cook for 2 minutes over low heat.

Add the milk and stir; simmer until thickened. Add the seasonings and simmer 2 additional minutes.

Combine the tomato mixture with the white sauce. Simmer for 10 minutes.

While sauce simmers, cook the pasta in 8 cups (2 L) of boiling salted water until al dente.

Plate the pasta, smother with sauce and serve.

SERVES 6

* Available in the specialty food section of your supermarket, or use any pasta of your choice.

Lemon Pepper Pasta

Ingredients:

1 tsp	5 ml	fresh cracked black pepper
2 tbsp	30 ml	grated lemon rind
3	3	eggs, beaten
2 cups	500 ml	all purpose flour
		ice water, only if required

Preparation:

In a mixing bowl, blend the pepper, lemon and eggs together. Add the flour slowly and knead into a soft dough ball (add small amounts of ice water, if required).

Knead the dough for 15 minutes and allow to rest for an additional 15 minutes. Roll out the dough. Lightly dust with flour, fold in three and roll out again. Repeat 6 to 8 times.

Now pass the dough through the pasta machine, setting the rollers gradually down until you reach the desired thickness. The result should be a smooth sheet of dough ready to process as you require.

SERVES 4

Chef's Corner

Lemon Pepper

Lemon Pepper is actually a blend of lemon zest, salt, pepper and other herbs or spices.

Spicy California Shrimp Pasta

Ingredients:

½ tsp	3 ml	each of oregano, basil, thyme, onion powder
1 tsp	5 ml	garlic powder
¼ tsp	1 ml	each of cayenne pepper, black pepper, white pepper
1 tsp	5 ml	chili powder
1 tsp	5 ml	salt
4 tbsp	60 ml	olive oil
3	3	minced ancho chilies
3	3	minced garlic cloves
2 cups	500 ml	tomato purée
1 lb	454 g	large peeled & de-veined shrimp
1 lb	454 g	pasta (your choice)

Preparation:

Blend all the seasonings together. Reserve 1 tbsp (15 ml) of seasoned blend.

Heat 1 tbsp (15 ml) of oil in a sauce pan. Sauté the chilies and garlic, add the tomato purée and half of the seasonings. Simmer 20 minutes.

Dust the shrimp with the remaining seasonings. Heat the remaining oil in a skillet to very hot. Fry the shrimp a few at a time for 2 minutes per side. Once complete reserve hot.

Cook the pasta al dente in a large kettle of boiling water. Drain the pasta and toss with half the sauce. Top with the shrimp, smother with the remaining sauce and serve.

SERVES 6

Cannelloni with Veal in
Shiitake Sauce

Ingredients:

1½ lbs	675 g	grocer purchased Basic Pasta Dough or 1 quantity of our recipe (see page 78)
6 tbsp	90 ml	unsalted butter
5 tbsp	75 ml	flour
2 cups	500 ml	chicken stock (see page 146)
1 cup	250 ml	milk
3 tbsp	45 ml	olive oil
1	1	minced onion
1	1	minced garlic clove
1 lb	454 g	ground veal
¼ lb	120 g	ground pork
½ tsp	3 ml	each of thyme leaves and oregano
1 tsp	5 ml	chopped fresh basil
1 cup	250 ml	tomatoes - chopped and seeded
2 oz	60 g	Shiitake mushrooms
½ cup	125 ml	half & half cream

Preparation:

Cut the pasta after processing into 6" squares. Cook the squares in 3 quarts (3 L) boiling water. Drain and rinse under cold water. Leave in the water.

In a small saucepan heat 3 tbsp (45 ml) of butter. Add 3 tbsp (45 ml) of flour. Cook for 2 minutes. Add 1 cup (250 ml) of chicken stock and the milk. Simmer until sauce is very thick. Allow to cool.

In a skillet heat the oil. Sauté the onion and garlic until tender. Add the veal, pork and seasoning. Sauté until meat is thoroughly cooked. Drain any fat. Add the tomatoes and cook until no liquid remains. Transfer the meat to a mixing bowl. Add 1 cup (250 ml) of the cooled sauce. Blend thoroughly. Lightly butter a large casserole dish. Pat dry the pasta. Place 2 tbsp (30 ml) of filling on each roll. Place the seam side down into the casserole dish. Repeat until complete.

Rehydrate the mushrooms by soaking in water. Drain and chop the mushrooms.

Heat the remaining butter in a sauce pan. Sauté the mushrooms for 2 minutes.

Add the remaining flour. Cook for an additional 2 minutes. Add the remaining chicken stock and cream. Whip in the remaining cooled sauce. Simmer until sauce is thickened. Pour over cannelloni.

Bake 20 minutes in a preheated 400°F (200°C) oven until very bubbly. Serve.

SERVES 8

NOTE: A shiitake mushroom is a Japanese mushroom available in Oriental food stores.

Seafood Orzo

Ingredients:

½ lb	225 g	clams
½ lb	225 g	mussels
¼ cup	60 ml	oil
1	1	diced onion
1	1	diced green bell pepper
3	3	diced celery stalks
2	2	minced garlic cloves
1 tsp	5 ml	each of thyme, oregano, basil, cracked black pepper
6 cups	1.5 L	chicken broth (see page 146)
2 cups	500 ml	white wine
2 cups	500 ml	crushed tomatoes
3 cups	750 ml	orzo
1 lb	454 g	crab legs & claws
1 lb	454 g	lobster meat
1 lb	454 g	peeled and de-veined shrimp
1 lb	454 g	firm fish pieces
1 cup	250 ml	peas

Preparation:

Preheat the oven to 375°F (190°C).

Clean and debeard the clams and mussels.

Heat the oil in a large kettle or Dutch oven. Add the onion, green pepper, celery and garlic. Sauté until the vegetables are tender, drain excess oil.

Add the seasonings and cook for 1 minute. Add the chicken broth, wine and tomatoes. Bring to a boil.

Place the orzo into a very large casserole dish. Top with the mussels, clams, crab, lobster, shrimp, fish and peas.

Pour the stock over the seafood, bake in the oven for 30 minutes or until the orzo is tender. Do not stir.

Remove from the oven. Cover and allow to sit for 10 minutes before serving.

SERVES 8

Tagliatelle Ai Funghi
E Vegtali

Ingredients:

4 tbsp	60 ml	butter
2 cups	500 ml	sliced button mushrooms
1	1	julienne cut carrot
1	1	small julienne cut zucchini
1½ cups	375 ml	rapini florets
4 tbsp	60 ml	all-purpose flour
1 cup	250 ml	milk
1 cup	250 ml	strong chicken broth (see page 146)
½ tsp	3 ml	salt
½ tsp	3 ml	white pepper
⅛ tsp	pinch	nutmeg
¼ cup	60 ml	hard Romano cheese, grated
1 lb	454 g	grocer purchased Tomato Tagliatelle Pasta

Preparation:

Melt the butter in a saucepan, add the vegetables and sauté until tender. Add flour and stir into a paste (roux) cook for 2 minutes over low heat.

Add the milk and chicken broth, stir; simmer until thickened. Add the seasonings and simmer 2 additional minutes. Add the cheese.

While sauce is simmering cook the pasta in 8 cups (2 L) of boiling salted water until al dente. Plate the noodles and smother with sauce.

SERVES 6

* Tagliatelle is a noodle approximately ½" (1.25 cm) wide, available in the pasta section of your supermarket.

Tomato Pasta Dough

Ingredients:

2	2	eggs
¼ cup	60 ml	tomato paste
1 tbsp	15 ml	olive oil
2 cups	500 ml	semolina flour
		ice water, only if required

Preparation:

Blend the eggs, tomato paste and oil together. Place in a mixing bowl. Slowly add the flour. Knead into a smooth ball (add ice water if required).

Knead the dough for 15 minutes and allow to rest for an additional 15 minutes. Roll out the dough. Lightly dust with flour, fold in three and roll out again. Repeat 6 to 8 times.

Now pass the dough through the pasta machine, setting the rollers gradually down until you reach the desired thickness. The result should be a smooth sheet of dough ready to process as you require.

Chef's Corner

Try using Parmesan or hardened Cacciocavallo instead of Romano.

Vegetable Canneloni

Ingredients:

¾ lb	340 g	grocer purchased Basic Pasta Dough or ½ quantity of our recipe (see page 78)
2 tbsp	30 ml	safflower oil
2	2	minced garlic cloves
1 cup	250 ml	fine julienne-cut zucchini
1 cup	250 ml	fine julienne-cut carrots
½ cup	125 ml	fine julienne-cut leeks
1 cup	250 ml	fine julienne-cut, pared apples
2	2	eggs, beaten
2 cups	500 ml	Ricotta cheese
2 tbsp	30 ml	chopped parsley
1 tbsp	15 ml	chopped basil leaves
1 cup	250 ml	grated Cheddar cheese
3 cups	750 ml	Tomato Sauce (see page 126)
½ cup	125 ml	freshly grated Romano cheese

Preparation:

Roll out the pasta as directed. Cut into 6" squares. Cook the pasta in a large kettle of boiling salted water. Drain and rinse in cold water. Leave in the water until required.

Heat the oil in a large skillet. Sauté the garlic, vegetables and apples in the oil until tender. Remove from heat, drain excess oil and moisture.

Beat together the eggs. Blend in the Ricotta cheese, herbs and Cheddar. Fold in the vegetables and apples.

Drain and pat dry the pasta. Place 2 tbsp (30 ml) of filling on each sheet. Roll together. Place in a lightly buttered large casserole dish seam side up.

Pour the Tomato Sauce over the canneloni. Sprinkle with the Romano.

Bake in a preheated 350°F (180°C) oven for 30-40 minutes. Serve.

SERVES 6

100

Garlic Cilantro Pesto Linguine

Ingredients:

¾ lb	340 g	grocer purchased Cilantro Pasta Dough or 1 quantity of our recipe
1 cup	250 ml	Ricotta cheese, room temperature
3	3	large minced garlic cloves
½ cup	125 ml	cleaned chopped cilantro
½ cup	125 ml	chopped fresh basil
½ cup	125 ml	hot chicken broth (see page 146)
⅓ cup	80 ml	fresh grated Cacciocavallo cheese

Preparation:

Process the pasta according to directions, cut into linguine noodles.

In a food processor combine the Ricotta cheese, garlic, cilantro, basil, broth and Cacciocavallo cheese, process until smooth.

Cook the pasta in 8 cups (2 L) of boiling salted water to al dente. Drain the linguine and toss with the pesto. Serve at once.

SERVES 4

Cilantro Pasta

Ingredients:

2	2	eggs, beaten
1 tsp	5 ml	safflower oil
½ cup	125 ml	chopped cilantro leaves
2 cups	500 ml	semolina flour
		ice water, only if required

Preparation:

Blend the eggs, oil and cilantro together. Add the flour and slowly knead into a soft ball (add small amounts of ice water if required).

Knead the dough for 15 minutes and allow to rest for an additional 15 minutes. Roll out the dough. Lightly dust with flour, fold in three and roll out again. Repeat 6 to 8 times.

Now pass the dough through the pasta machine, setting the rollers gradually down until you reach the desired thickness. The result should be a smooth sheet of dough ready to process as you require.

SERVES 6

Chef's Corner

Cilantro

Cilantro is also known as fresh coriander or Chinese parsley.

Oriental Spicy Chicken

Ingredients:

3 tbsp	45 ml	peanut oil
½ lb	225 g	diced raw chicken
2	2	minced garlic cloves
1 tsp	5 ml	minced ginger root
½ tsp	3 ml	red pepper flakes
½ cup	125 ml	sliced mushrooms
1 cup	250 ml	finely diced cabbage
½ cup	125 ml	chicken broth (see page 146)
1 tsp	5 ml	cornstarch
2 tbsp	30 ml	soy sauce
¾ lb	340 g	grocer purchased Egg Pasta or 1 quantity of our recipe (see page 122)

Preparation:

In a wok or large skillet, heat the oil. Sauté the chicken until it is cooked thoroughly. Add the garlic, ginger and red pepper flakes, cook for 1 minute. Add the mushrooms, cabbage and chicken broth. Simmer for 5 minutes.

Mix the cornstarch with the soy sauce. Add to the chicken and simmer until thicken.

While the chicken cooks, boil 2 quarts (2 L) of salted water in a large kettle. Add the noodles. Simmer for 3 minutes. Drain. Transfer to a serving plate.

Pour the chicken over the noodles. Serve at once.

SERVES 6

Red Wine Mushroom Beef Spaghetti

Ingredients:

1 lb	454 g	grocer purchased Basic Pasta Dough or 1 quantity of our recipe (see page 78)
2¼ lbs	1 kg	sirloin, sliced into thin strips
3 tbsp	45 ml	butter
3 tbsp	45 ml	safflower oil
1	1	diced small Spanish onion
3	3	minced garlic cloves
4 oz	115 g	sliced mushrooms
3 tbsp	45 ml	finely diced carrots
3 tbsp	45 ml	finely diced celery
¼ cup	60 ml	all-purpose flour
½ cup	125 ml	red wine
2 cups	500 ml	beef broth (see page 82)
3 tbsp	45 ml	tomato paste
1 tsp	5 ml	each of black pepper, garlic powder, onion powder
¼ cup	60 ml	freshly grated Romano cheese

Preparation:

Process the pasta as directed and cut into spaghetti noodles.

In a large Dutch oven or kettle, sauté the beef in the butter and oil. Add the vegetables and continue to cook until tender. Sprinkle with the flour, reduce the heat and cook for 5 minutes.

Add the wine, broth, tomato paste and seasonings. Simmer for 50 minutes covered.

While the sauce is simmering cook the pasta al dente in 8 cups (2 L) of boiling salted water. Drain, place on serving plates, smother with sauce and sprinkle with the Romano cheese.

SERVES 6

Fettucini Alla Dianna

Ingredients:

4 tbsp	60 ml	butter
4 tbsp	60 ml	all-purpose flour
2 cups	500 ml	milk
½ tsp	3 ml	salt
½ tsp	3 ml	white pepper
pinch	pinch	nutmeg
2 cups	500 ml	flaked, cooked salmon (do not use tinned)
1 cup	250 ml	diced mangoes
1 lb	454 g	fettucini
¼ cup	60 ml	grated Parmesan cheese

Preparation:

Melt the butter in a saucepan. Add flour and stir into a paste (roux). Cook for 2 minutes over low heat.

Add the milk and stir. Simmer until thickened. Add the seasonings and simmer for 2 additional minutes. Stir in the salmon, mangoes and cheese. Simmer for an additional 5 minutes.

While sauce simmers, cook the fettucini in 8 cups (2 L) of boiling salted water to al dente. Drain the noodles and smother with sauce. Serve.

SERVES 6

Chef's Corner

Safflower Oil

When given the choice of safflower or peanut oil, choose safflower. Safflower has a high smoking point which makes it perfect for deep frying, as does peanut oil. However, safflower is tasteless. This means that the taste of the item cooked in it is preserved. In addition, safflower tends not to transfer flavors of other items cooked in it. Safflower is also an excellent oil to use when blending oils for salad dressings. ⅓ safflower to ⅔ olive oil will make a wonderful blend for use in a dressing for greens.

Shrimp & Lobster Lo Mein

Ingredients:

3 tbsp	45 ml	peanut oil
½ lb	225 g	shrimp meat
½ lb	225 g	diced lobster meat
1	1	finely diced scallion
1 cup	250 ml	finely sliced mushroom
1 lb	454 g	blanched green beans
1 cup	250 ml	chicken stock (see page 146)
1 tbsp	15 ml	honey
1 tbsp	15 ml	soy sauce
1 tsp	5 ml	cornstarch
¾ lb	340 g	grocer purchased Egg Pasta Dough or 1 quantity of our recipe (see page 122)

Preparation:

In a wok or large skillet heat the oil. Sauté the shrimp and lobster until cooked through. Add the scallion, mushrooms and green beans. Fry 1 minute.

Add the chicken stock. Simmer for 3 minutes. Mix the honey with the soy sauce. Blend in the cornstarch. Add to the seafood and simmer for 2 minutes.

In a large kettle boil 2 quarts (2 L) of salted water, cook noodles for 3 minutes. Drain. Transfer to a serving plate. Pour seafood over noodles. Serve.

SERVES 6

Linguine Romano

Ingredients:

¾ lb	345 g	grocer purchased Pasta Verde Dough or 1 quantity of our recipe
3	3	minced garlic cloves
1 tbsp	15 ml	chopped fresh thyme leaves
½ cup	125 ml	chopped arugula leaves
1 tbsp	15 ml	chopped fresh basil leaves
4 tbsp	60 ml	olive oil
½ cup	125 ml	Romano cheese

Preparation:

Prepare the pasta as directed. Cut into linguine. Cook in a large kettle of boiling salted water. Drain.

In a food processor or blender, purée the garlic, thyme, arugula and basil. Add the oil and Romano cheese. Blend another 10 seconds. Toss the hot noodles in the pesto. Serve.

SERVES 6

Pasta Verde

Ingredients:

1 ½ lbs	625 g	fresh spinach
3 cups	750 ml	semolina flour
4	4	eggs, beaten
		ice water, only if required

Preparation:

Wash and rinse the spinach well. Chop the spinach fine. Blend the flour and spinach together. Slowly add the flour into the eggs. Knead into a smooth ball (add small amounts of ice water if required).

Knead the dough for 15 minutes and allow to rest for an additional 15 minutes. Roll out the dough. Lightly dust with flour, fold in three and roll out again. Repeat 6 to 8 times.

Now pass the dough through the pasta machine, setting the rollers gradually down until you reach the desired thickness. The result should be a smooth sheet of dough ready to process as you require.

SERVES 6

Chef's Corner

If you choose to substitute dried herbs for fresh, use ⅓ less.

Fettucine with Mushrooms, Shrimp, Olive Oil, Garlic, and Fresh Herbs

Ingredients:

3 tbsp	45 ml	butter
1 lb	454 g	large peeled and de-veined shrimp
¼ lb	120 g	sliced mushrooms
3	3	minced garlic cloves
1 tbsp	15 ml	chopped fresh thyme leaves
2 tbsp	30 ml	chopped cilantro leaves
1 tbsp	15 ml	chopped fresh basil leaves
4 tbsp	60 ml	olive oil
1½ lbs	675 g	colored fettucine noodles

Preparation:

Heat the butter in a large skillet, add the shrimp and mushrooms and sauté for 6 minutes, reserve hot.

In a food processor or blender, purée the garlic, thyme, cilantro and basil. Add the oil. Blend another 10 seconds.

Cook the pasta in a large kettle of boiling salted water. Drain and place in a large serving bowl.

Toss the hot noodles, shrimp and mushrooms in the pesto. Serve.

SERVES 6

Orecchiette
in Tomato Cream

Ingredients:

1½ lbs	675 g	grocer purchased Cornmeal Pasta Dough or 1 quantity of our recipe
1	1	red bell pepper
2 tbsp	30 ml	butter
1	1	diced onion
1	1	minced garlic clove
½ tsp	3 ml	each of salt, basil and thyme
1 tsp	5 ml	cracked black pepper
2 tbsp	30 ml	all-purpose flour
½ cup	125 ml	half & half cream
¼ cup	60 ml	sherry
1½ cups	375 ml	stewed tomatoes

Preparation:

To make orecchiette (little ears) divide the pasta in half. Roll into a long rope shape and cut into ⅛" (3 mm) thick rounds. Dust each with flour. Place a round in the palm of your hand and indent the centre with your finger. Repeat until all rounds are complete.

Wrap the red pepper in foil. Bake in a preheated 400°F (200°C) oven for 15 minutes. Remove the foil and peel away the skin from the pepper. Core and seed the pepper. Fine dice the pepper.

Heat the butter in a saucepan. Sauté the onion with the garlic until tender. Add the seasonings and red bell pepper, cook for 5-7 minutes. Sprinkle with the flour and continue to cook for an additional 2 minutes over low heat.

Add the cream and sherry and simmer until thick. Add the tomatoes, continue simmering for an additional 10 minutes.

While the sauce is simmering, cook the pasta in 3 quarts (3 L) of boiling salted water for approximately 9 minutes. Drain and transfer to a serving bowl. Toss with the sauce and serve.

SERVES 6

Cornmeal Pasta

Ingredients:

1½ cups	375 ml	fine ground cornmeal
1½ cups	375 ml	semolina flour
4	4	eggs, beaten
1 tbsp	15 ml	safflower oil
		ice water, only if required

Preparation:

Blend the cornmeal and flour together. Beat the oil with the eggs. Place in a mixing bowl. Slowly add the flour. Knead into a smooth ball (add small amounts of ice water if required).

Knead the dough for 15 minutes and allow to rest for an additional 15 minutes. Roll out the dough. Lightly dust with flour, fold in three and roll out again. Repeat 6 to 8 times.

Now pass the dough through the pasta machine, setting the rollers gradually down until you reach the desired thickness. The result should be a smooth sheet of dough ready to process as you require.

SERVES 6

Chef's Corner

Have your oven checked by a professional service person at least once a year to ensure the temperature calibration is correct.

Turkey Tortellini

Ingredients:

10 oz	300 g	grocer purchased Lemon Pepper Pasta or 1 quantity of our recipe (see page 90)
1 tbsp	15 ml	butter
1	1	minced small carrot
1	1	minced celery stalk
8 oz	225 g	minced smoked turkey
½ cup	125 ml	Ricotta cheese
¼ tsp	1 ml	dried thyme leaves
¼ tsp	1 ml	dried basil leaves
1	1	egg
½ cup	125 ml	dry sherry
¼ cup	60 ml	tomato paste
1½ cups	375 ml	chicken broth (see page 146)
¼ cup	60 ml	freshly grated Romano cheese
2 tsp	10 ml	green peppercorns
1 tbsp	15 ml	chopped parsley

Preparation:

Process the pasta as directed. Roll into thin sheets. Cut the pasta in squares. Cover with a damp cloth and reserve.

Heat the butter in a skillet. Sauté the carrot and celery until tender. Place into a mixing bowl and cool to room temperature. Blend in the turkey, thyme, basil, egg and cooled vegetables, together in a food processor.

Place 1 teaspoon (5 ml) of filling on each square. Place a second square on top, moisten the edges with a little water. Fold the pasta square in half. Press the edges to seal. Cook the pasta in a large kettle of boiling, salted water for 2 minutes, after they float to the top.

For the sauce, place the sherry in a saucepan. Whip in the tomato paste and broth. Simmer to reduce to ⅔ volume. Whip in the cheese, peppercorns and parsley. Toss in the tortellini and serve.

SERVES 4

116

117

Triple Cheese Gnocchi

Ingredients:

1 lb	454 g	potatoes
¼ lb	125 g	freshly grated Cheddar cheese
½ lb	225 g	Ricotta cheese
1 cup	250 ml	freshly grated Romano cheese
2	2	eggs, beaten
1 ½ cups	375 ml	all purpose flour

Preparation:

Pare and steam the potatoes until they are fork tender. Purée.

Blend the cheeses together.

Blend the potatoes, cheeses and eggs together. Add the flour slowly. Knead, creating a soft dough. Mold the dough into teaspoon size pieces. Place on a floured surface and press with a fork.

Drop the dumplings into salted, boiling water. Cook for 3 minutes after the dumplings float. Serve with any variety of sauces. Mushroom Mornay Sauce is excellent.

SERVES 6

Mushroom Mornay Sauce

Ingredients:

3 tbsp	45 ml	butter
2 cups	500 ml	sliced button mushrooms
3 tbsp	45 ml	all purpose flour
1 ¼ cups	310 ml	chicken broth (see page 146)
1 ¼ cups	310 ml	half & half cream
½ cup	125 ml	freshly grated Parmesan cheese

Preparation:

Heat the butter in a saucepan. Add the mushrooms. Sauté until all the moisture has evaporated. Add the flour. Cook for 2 minutes over low heat. Stir in the chicken broth and cream. Reduce heat and simmer until thickened. Stir in the cheese and simmer for 2 more minutes.

Use as required.

YIELDS 3 cups (750 ml)

Chef's Corner

Romano (row-man-o):

A hard circular cheese 10 " (25 cm) in diameter and 7-9" (17-22 cm) in height with a greenish black surface and yellowish interior. Romano is made from a combination of cow's and goat's milk. It has cooking use and can be grated.

Fettucini Chicken Jambalaya

Ingredients:

1 ½ lbs	670 g	diced boneless chicken
2 tbsp	30 ml	safflower oil
2 tbsp	30 ml	butter
½ lb	225 g	andouille sausage (or any hot sausage)
½ cup	125 ml	diced onions
2	2	minced garlic cloves
3 tbsp	45 ml	chopped parsley
1 ½ cups	375 ml	diced green bell peppers
2	2	diced celery stalks
2 cups	500 ml	peeled, seeded and chopped tomatoes
1 tsp	3 ml	each of white pepper, black pepper, oregano leaves, basil, thyme leaves, garlic powder, onion powder, chili powder
2 tsp	10 ml	Worcestershire sauce
3 drops	3 drops	Tabasco™ sauce
1 lb	454 g	Fettucini noodles

Preparation:

In a Dutch oven or large kettle, sauté the chicken in the oil and butter. Add the sausage and vegetables. Continue to sauté until vegetables are tender.

Stir in the remaining ingredients (except pasta). Reduce heat. Cover and simmer on low heat for 40-45 minutes.

Cook the fettucini to al dente in 8 cups (2 L) boiling salted water. Drain. Place on a serving platter. Pour chicken on the noodles and serve.

SERVES 6

Spicy Broccoli Noodles

Ingredients:

1 lb	454 g	grocer purchased Egg Pasta or 1 quantity of our recipe
2 cups	500 ml	broccoli florets
1 tbsp	15 ml	peanut oil
2	2	small red peppers
1	1	minced garlic clove
1 tsp	5 ml	minced ginger root
½ lb	225 g	thin sliced flank steak
3 tbsp	45 ml	oyster sauce

Preparation:

Cook the noodles in a large kettle of salted boiling water. Drain and transfer to a serving plate. Reserve hot.

Blanch the broccoli in boiling water for 2 minutes.

In a wok or large skillet heat the oil, add the peppers, and cook until peppers turn black. Remove the peppers and discard, add the garlic and ginger and fry until golden brown. Add the steak and quickly fry. Add the broccoli. Fry for 1 minute. Add the oyster sauce. Fry for 1 additional minute .

Pour the beef over the noodles and serve at once.

SERVES 6

Egg Pasta

Ingredients:

3	3	eggs
2 cups	500 ml	semolina flour

Preparation:

Beat the eggs well. Slowly add the flour. Knead for 10 minutes. Cover and allow to rest for 15 minutes. Knead a second time. On a lightly floured, dusted board, roll very thin. Dust with flour. Fold and roll again. Repeat this several times. The result will be a smooth sheet of dough. Roll the dough and cut into very thin strips.

In a kettle, boil 2 quarts (2 L) of water.

Cook the noodles for 2-3 minutes.

Serve as desired.

SERVES 6

Chef's Corner

Try using broccoflower or rapini instead of broccoli.

Jumbo Veal Ravioli
with Basil Sauce

Ingredients:

2 tbsp	30 ml	olive oil
2	2	minced garlic cloves
1	1	diced green bell pepper
1	1	diced onion
2	2	diced celery stalks
4 oz	120 g	sliced mushrooms
1 tsp	5 ml	salt
½ tsp	3 ml	pepper
2 tbsp	30 ml	fresh basil leaves
3 lbs	1½ kg	peeled, seeded, and chopped tomatoes
1 lb	454 g	grocer purchased Cracked Black Pepper Pasta or 1 quantity of our recipe (see page 74)
1 tbsp	15 ml	olive oil
1 cup	250 ml	minced onion
½ cup	125 ml	minced green bell peppers
1	1	minced garlic clove
1 lb	454 g	raw ground veal
½ lb	225 g	hot or spicy Italian sausage meat
½ cup	125 ml	bread crumbs
2	2	eggs
¼ tsp	1 ml	oregano
⅛ tsp	pinch	cayenne pepper

Preparation:

In a sauce pan heat the oil. Sauté the garlic, green pepper, onion, celery and mushrooms until tender. Add the seasonings and tomatoes. Simmer for 3 hours or until desired thickness.

Prepare the pasta according to directions. Roll thin. Cover with a moist cloth until required.

Heat the oil in a skillet, sauté the onion, bell peppers and garlic until tender and all moisture has evaporated. Cool.

Blend the veal, sausage, bread crumbs, sautéed vegetables, eggs and seasonings together.

On a pasta sheet place 1 tbsp (15 ml) size of filling spread evenly over the sheet. Lightly moisten the pasta around the filling. Place a second sheet of pasta over the first. Use a scalloped pastry roll and cut between the filling.

Place the ravioli in a kettle of salted boiling water a few at a time. Cook for 3-4 minutes after each floats. Transfer to a serving platter, smother with the sauce and serve.

SERVES 6

Chef's Corner

Tomatoes

To ripen a tomato place it in a paper bag along with an apple. The apple will produce a gas that will speed up the tomato's ripening process naturally. Tomatoes can be frozen if placed on a cookie sheet before freezing. Once frozen place in a plastic bag. They will keep 4-6 months. Thaw by running under warm water. This will also remove the skin. Frozen tomatoes cannot be used as one would use a fresh tomato. However, they are excellent for use in soups, sauces and stews.

Baked Yellow Peppers
With Orzo

Ingredients:

½ lb	225 g	orzo
2 tsp	10 ml	safflower oil
½ lb	225 g	hot Italian sausage meat
3	3	small minced garlic cloves
2	2	finely diced shallots
1	1	finely diced celery stalk
1 tsp	5 ml	chopped fresh thyme
1 tsp	5 ml	chopped fresh basil
1 tbsp	15 ml	chopped fresh parsley
¼ cup	60 ml	finely diced scallions
½ cup	125 ml	grated Parmesan cheese
2 cups	500 ml	chicken broth (see page 146)
4 oz	115 g	grated Provolone cheese
6	6	medium yellow bell peppers
3 tsp	15 ml	dry bread crumbs
2 cups	500 ml	hot Tomato Sauce

Preparation:

Prepare the orzo according to package directions; drain and set aside.

Heat the oil in a medium sauce pan, fry the sausage until cooked through. Add the garlic, shallots and celery and sauté until tender.

Stir in orzo, thyme, basil, parsley, scallions, Parmesan cheese, ½ cup (125 ml) of the chicken broth and half the Provolone cheese.

Preheat the oven to 350°F (180°C).

Cut the tops off the peppers and remove the seeds. Cut a small piece off the bottom of each pepper so they will stand up. Spoon the pasta mixture into each of the peppers and then set the peppers in a baking dish. Sprinkle ½ tsp (3 ml) of bread crumbs on top of each pepper. Sprinkle the remaining Provolone cheese over top of each pepper. Pour the remaining 1½ cups (375 ml) of chicken broth around the peppers. Bake for 45 minutes, until the peppers are brown on top and very tender.

Place a small amount of Tomato Sauce on serving plates. Place a pepper on top of the sauce and serve at once.

SERVES 6

Tomato Sauce
Ingredients:

¼ cup	60 ml	butter
2	2	minced garlic cloves
2	2	diced carrots
1	1	diced onion
2	2	diced celery stalks
3¼ lbs	1.5 kg	peeled, seeded and chopped tomatoes
3	3	bay leaves
1 tsp	5 ml	dried thyme leaves
1 tsp	5 ml	dried oregano leaves
1 tsp	5 ml	dried basil leaves
1 tbsp	15 ml	salt
1 tsp	5 ml	pepper

Preparation:

In a large kettle heat the butter. Sauté the garlic, carrots, onion and celery until tender. Add the tomatoes and seasonings. Reduce heat and simmer for 3 hours.

Strain the sauce and return to the pot continuing to simmer to desired thickness.

YIELDS 4 cups (1 L)

Chef's Corner

Parmesan

A cylindrical, hard cheese with a dark green surface and yellowish-white interior. It is used in grated form, most commonly to top a plate of pasta.

Cajun Seafood Linguine

Ingredients:

⅓ cup	80 ml	butter
¾ cup	180 ml	diced onions
1	1	diced green bell pepper
2 cups	500 ml	peeled, seeded and diced tomatoes
1 tsp	5 ml	each of salt, pepper, paprika
½ tsp	3 ml	each of oregano leaves, thyme leaves, cayenne pepper, garlic powder, onion powder, chili powder
1 tsp	5 ml	Worcestershire sauce
5 drops	5 drops	Tabasco™ sauce
¼ cup	60 ml	chopped green onions
2 tbsp	30 ml	chopped parsley
1 lb	454 g	peeled and de-veined shrimp
½ lb	225 g	peeled crayfish tails
½ lb	225 g	diced catfish fillets
1 lb	454 g	linguine noodles

Preparation:

Melt the butter in a saucepan. Add the onion and pepper. Sauté until tender. Add the tomatoes, seasonings, Worcestershire and Tabasco™. Reduce the heat and simmer for 30 minutes.

Add the green onions, parsley, shrimp, crayfish and catfish. Cover and simmer for 10 minutes.

Cook the linguine in 8 cups (2 L) of boiling salted water until al dente. Drain and transfer to a serving plate. Cover with etouffée and serve at once.

SERVES 6

Oyster Rockefeller Manicotti

Ingredients:

1½ lbs	675 g	grocer purchased Basic Pasta Dough or 1 quantity of our recipe (see page 78)
36	36	oysters
10 oz	300 g	spinach
4 tbsp	60 ml	butter
2	2	minced celery stalks
6	6	minced green onions
½ cup	125 ml	chopped parsley
¼ cup	60 ml	bread crumbs
1 tbsp	15 ml	Worcestershire sauce
3 drops	3 drops	Tabasco™ sauce
¼ tsp	1 ml	salt (optional)
¼ cup	60 ml	freshly grated Parmesan cheese,
2 cups	500 ml	Ricotta cheese
2 cups	500 ml	Mornay Sauce (see page 12)

Preparation:

Process the pasta as directed. Roll into thin sheets. Cut the pasta sheets into 4" squares. Cook the sheets of dough al dente in boiling salted water. Drain and run cool water over the sheets. Reserve. Shuck the oysters. Reserve the oyster nectar.

Trim the spinach and chop coarsely. Heat the butter in a skillet. Sauté the oysters and spinach until the oysters are cooked through. Remove the oysters and spinach. Reserve.

Sauté the celery, green onions and parsley for 2 minutes. Mix with the oysters. Blend in the remaining ingredients, except the Mornay Sauce, with the oysters. Place filling on pasta. Roll together. Place the manicotti in a lightly buttered casserole pan, seam side down. Pour the Mornay Sauce over.

Bake in a 350°F (180°C) oven for 30 minutes. Serve.

SERVES 6

* Very nice with Spanish Caesar Salad.

Spanish Caesar Salad

Ingredients:

1	1	garlic clove
2	2	egg yolks
1 tsp	5 ml	dry mustard
2 tsp	10 ml	granulated sugar
⅛ tsp	pinch	cayenne pepper
1½ cups	375 ml	olive oil
3 tbsp	45 ml	lemon juice
¼ cup	60 ml	buttermilk
⅓ cup	80 ml	freshly grated Parmesan cheese
2 tbsp	30 ml	minced chives
3	3	seeded, finely diced jalapeño peppers
½ tsp	3 ml	cracked black pepper
2	2	heads, washed Romaine lettuce
⅓ cup	80 ml	diced cooked bacon
⅓ cup	80 ml	croutons

Preparation:

Place the garlic, egg yolks, mustard, sugar and cayenne in a blender or food processor. With the machine running, very slowly, add the oil in a thin stream until mixture reaches the consistency of mayonnaise. Stir in the lemon juice, buttermilk, cheese, chives, jalapeños and pepper. Cut the lettuce into bite size pieces and place into a large bowl. Cover lettuce with the dressing and toss to coat.

Serve the salad on chilled plates. Garnish with bacon and croutons.

SERVES 6

Seafood Vegetable Lasagna

Ingredients:

½ lb	225 g	mafalda* noodles
3 tbsp	45 ml	butter
2 tbsp	30 ml	olive oil
½ cup	125 ml	diced carrots
1	1	diced small onion
1	1	diced red bell pepper
2	2	diced celery stalks
3 tbsp	45 ml	flour
½ cup	125 ml	peas
1 cup	250 ml	broccoli florets
1 cup	250 ml	chicken broth (see page 146)
½ cup	125 ml	whipping cream
⅓ cup	80 ml	freshly grated Parmesan cheese
1 tsp	5 ml	salt
½ tsp	3 ml	cracked black pepper
1½ cups	375 ml	seafood, shrimp or crab or lobster or combination
1½ cups	375 ml	grated Cheddar cheese
⅓ cup	80 ml	freshly grated Romano cheese

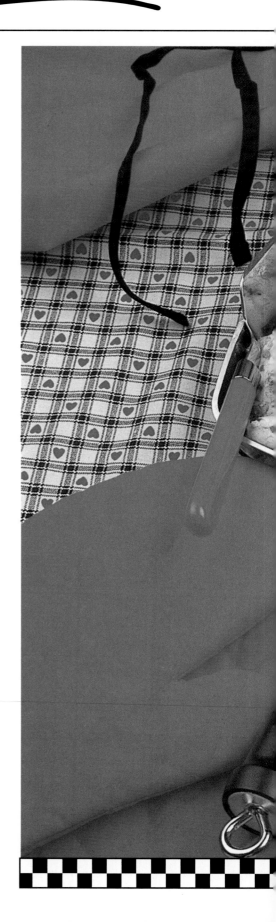

Preparation:

In a large kettle of boiling salted water, cook the noodles. Drain and rinse under cold water. Place in a large greased casserole pan.

Heat the butter and the oil together. Sauté the carrots, onion, pepper and celery until tender. Sprinkle with flour. Cook for 2 minutes. Add the peas, broccoli, broth and cream. Simmer until thick. Add cheese, seasonings and seafood. Pour over noodles.

Sprinkle with Cheddar and Romano. Bake for 20 minutes in a preheated 375°F (190°C) oven. Serve.

SERVES 4

*Mafalda is a noodle (2 ½ cm) 1" wide, available in the pasta section of the supermarket.

Fennel and Italian Sausage,
Prosciutto & Orzo

Ingredients:

3 tbsp	45 ml	herbed olive oil
1 tbsp	30 ml	butter
1 cup	250 ml	chopped onion
1	1	chopped red bell pepper
6	6	minced garlic cloves
½ cup	125 ml	chopped fennel
8 oz	225 g	Italian sausages, removed from casings
4 oz	115 g	minced prosciutto
1 tsp	5 ml	salt
½ tsp	3 ml	cracked black pepper
1 cup	250 ml	orzo
¾ cup	180 ml	white wine
3 cups	750 ml	chicken broth (see page 146)
¾ cup	180 ml	freshly grated Parmesan cheese

Preparation:

Heat the oil and butter in a large saucepan and sauté the onions and bell pepper. Mix in the garlic, fennel, and sausage, breaking the sausage. Season with salt and pepper.

Add the orzo and sauté for 1 minute, making sure that the orzo is well coated with oil.

Heat the wine and broth together and add to the orzo in thirds allowing the orzo to absorb the liquid before adding the next third. When orzo has absorbed all the liquid remove from the heat and stir in the Parmesan cheese.

SERVES 4

Chef's Corner

Onion

It's the vegetable that makes every dish worth crying over. Onions have become a mainstay in every area of cuisine, except that of desserts. Onions are a member of the lily family as are garlic, chives and leeks.

Onions can be found as shallots or small multiple clove onions that are somewhat milder in taste than the larger varieties. Scallions (green onions) are long, slender, tender and mild in flavor. They are excellent in soups and sauces.

Bermudas are the most common of the large onions sold. Mild to strong in flavor, they are available in white, yellow and red colors. Spanish onions much like Bermudas, are mild in taste and very large in size. These are available in white and yellow. Silverskins are smaller in size than the Bermudas but are very strong in flavor.

Pearl or Button onions are very small and are found in red and white varieties. They are often used in stews, blanquettes and other similar dishes. Vidalia onions are similar to Bermudas. However, they are very sweet and should be used in dishes that require mild flavoring.

The biggest problem with onions is that they release an irritant that bothers the eyes and causes tearing. There are as many ways to prevent this as there are varieties of onions- none of which is valid in stopping the tears. Some more useful remedies include using a very sharp knife as a dull knife bruises the skin and releases more irritant or trying to keep the onion moist but not wet so it doesn't slip and bruise while you cut it.

Chicken Manicotti

Ingredients:

¾ lb	340 g	grocer purchased Basic Pasta Dough, or ½ quantity of our recipe (see page 78)
10 oz	230 g	package frozen chopped spinach, thawed and drained
½ lb	225 g	Ricotta cheese
½ lb	225 g	Mascarpone cheese
½ cup	125 ml	grated Parmesan cheese
2	2	large eggs
2½ cups	625 ml	diced cooked chicken breast
1 tbsp	15 ml	chopped fresh basil
1 tsp	5 ml	pepper
3 tbsp	45 ml	butter
3 tbsp	45 ml	all-purpose flour
1 cup	250 ml	chicken broth (see page 146)
1 cup	250 ml	half & half cream
¼ cup	60 ml	grated Romano cheese

Preparation:

Process the pasta as directed and cut for 12 manicotti tubes. Cook the pasta in 8 cups (2 L) of boiling salted water. Drain and cool under cold water.

While pasta is cooking, squeeze all the water out of the spinach.

Preheat the oven to 350°F (180°C).

Mix together the spinach, Ricotta, Mascarpone, Parmesan, eggs, chicken, basil and pepper. Spoon the cheese mixture onto the manicotti shells, roll together and lay seam side down in a 9 x 13-inch pan.

Melt the butter in a small saucepan, add the flour and cook for 2 minutes over low heat. Add the chicken broth and cream, simmer until very thick. Pour over the manicotti, sprinkle with Romano cheese. Cover and bake 20 minutes. Remove cover and bake an additional 15 minutes, until cheese is golden brown.

SERVES 6

Spicy Summer Pasta Salad

Ingredients:

8 oz	225 g	multi-colored Rotini
1 cup	250 ml	fresh green beans, cut into 1" (2.5 cm) pieces, blanched
2	2	sliced small zucchini
2	2	sliced small yellow squash
1 cup	250 ml	thinly sliced carrots
1	1	medium red onion, cut into eighths
1 ½ cups	375 ml	Ailloli
¼ cup	60 ml	chopped fresh basil leaves
½ cup	125 ml	chopped oil-packed sun-dried tomatoes
¼ cup	60 ml	grated Parmesan cheese
1 ¼ tsp	6 ml	red pepper flakes
		salt and pepper to taste
¼ cup	60 ml	chopped fresh parsley

Preparation:

Prepare the pasta according to package directions; drain and cool under cold water.

In a large serving bowl, toss together the green beans, zucchini, squash, carrots, and onion.

Blend the pasta and the vegetables. Bind the salad together with the Ailloli.

Mix in the basil and sun-dried tomatoes, Parmesan cheese, and the red pepper flakes.

Taste and adjust seasoning with the salt and pepper, garnish with the parsley and serve.

SERVES 4

Ailloli

Ingredients:

2	2	garlic cloves, pounded into a paste
2	2	egg yolks
½ tsp	3 ml	salt
pinch	pinch	pepper
½ tsp	3 ml	Dijon mustard
1 cup	250 ml	olive oil
4 tsp	20 ml	wine vinegar

Preparation:

In a blender or food processor cream the garlic, egg yolks, salt, pepper and mustard.

With the machine running add the oil in a slow thin stream. Add the vinegar.

Pour into a serving bowl or use as required.

YIELDS 1 ½ cups (375ml)

Chef's Corner

Orzo

Orzo is a dried pasta shaped like rice found in the pasta section of your grocery store.

Cous Cous Zucchini Salad

Ingredients:

1	1	garlic clove
2	2	egg yolks
1 tsp	5 ml	dry mustard
2 tsp	10 ml	sugar
⅛ tsp	pinch	cayenne pepper
1½ cups	375 ml	olive oil
3 tbsp	45 ml	lemon juice
¼ cup	60 ml	buttermilk
⅓ cup	80 ml	freshly grated Parmesan cheese
2 tbsp	30 ml	minced chives
½ tsp	3 ml	cracked black pepper
2 cups	500 ml	cous cous
1 cup	250 ml	finely diced zucchini
3	3	peeled, seeded and chopped tomatoes
6	6	finely chopped green onions

Preparation:

Place the garlic, egg yolks, mustard, sugar and cayenne in a blender or food processor. With the machine running, very slowly add the oil in a thin stream until mixture reaches the consistency of mayonnaise. Stir in the lemon juice, buttermilk, Parmesan cheese, chives and pepper.

Cook the cous cous. Drain and chill. Place into a mixing bowl and add the vegetables.

Pour the dressing over the salad. Chill for 2½ hours. Serve.

SERVES 8

NOTE: This salad will not keep well overnight. It should be served immediately after refrigeration.

Curried Veal Fettucini

Ingredients:

1½ lbs	675 g	veal, shoulder diced in ¾" (1.8 cm) cubes
4 cups	1 L	chicken stock (see page 146)
2 tsp	10 ml	salt
20	20	pearl onions
4	4	carrots, julienned
2 tbsp	30 ml	butter
2 tbsp	30 ml	all purpose flour
2 tbsp	30 ml	curry powder
2 tbsp	30 ml	lemon juice
2	2	egg yolks
1 lb	454 g	fettucini noodles
1 tbsp	15 ml	chopped parsley

Preparation:

In a Dutch oven place the veal, chicken stock and salt. Cover and simmer for 1½ hours. Add the onions and carrots. Continue cooking for 15 minutes. Remove 2 cups (500 ml) of liquid.

Melt the butter in a small sauce pan. Add the flour and curry powder. Cook for 3 minutes over low heat. Slowly add the 2 cups (500 ml) of liquid, stirring until thickened.

Whisk the lemon juice in the egg yolks and blend into the sauce. **Do not boil**.

Boil 12 cups (3 L) of salted water. Cook the fettucini noodles al dente. Drain and transfer to a serving platter.

Add the sauce to the veal. Reheat but do not boil. Pour onto the noodles and garnish with the parsley. Serve at once.

SERVES 6

Chef's Corner

Edible Flowers

Today, many cooks have realized the advantages of using edible flowers, not only to enhance their final plates but also as a flavor enhancing herb.

You may use any of the following:

Butterblossom summer squash - has a mild flavor of the squash from which it is picked.

Calendula, pot marigold - has a slight mild pepper flavor. Enhances soups and salads.

Carnation - has a mild flavor. It is usually available year round, and comes in a great variety of colors that will complement any dish.

Dianthus - has a mild clove flavor. Available in pink, rose, red and white.

Johnny-Jump Ups - have a mild wintergreen flavor, found in yellow, violet and lavender. Excellent with fruit and ice creams.

Marigold - has a slight lemon flavor. Use it in exchange for saffron, as Marigolds are far less expensive.

Nasturtium - has a strong peppery flavor and is probably the most popular of edible flowers.

Canary Creeper - part of the nasturtium family, resembling tiny birds. Perfect on dishes with fruit sauces.

Sweet violet - has a wintergreen flavor and is violet in color. An excellent garnish for desserts as the taste is slightly sweet.

Rapini, Rotini Vegetable Salad

Ingredients:

2	2	garlic cloves
2	2	egg yolks
½ tsp	3 ml	salt
⅛ tsp	pinch	pepper
½ tsp	3 ml	Dijon mustard
1 cup	250 ml	olive oil
4 tsp	20 ml	wine vinegar
1 cup	250 ml	rapini
1 cup	250 ml	cauliflower buds
1	1	julienne cut large carrot
1	1	julienne cut celery stalk
1	1	julienne cut red bell pepper
1 cup	250 ml	peel, seeded and chopped tomatoes
4	4	chopped green onions
4 cups	1 L	cooked rotini
1 cup	250 ml	grated Cheddar

Preparation:

In a blender or food processor cream the garlic, egg yolks, salt, pepper and mustard.

With the machine running add the oil in a slow thin stream. Add the vinegar.

In a large salad bowl mix the vegetables with the rotini.

Pour the dressing over the salad and mix thoroughly. Place into chilled serving bowls, sprinkle with the Cheddar cheese and serve.

SERVES 6

Oregano Chicken Pasta Pleaser

Ingredients:

1½ lbs	675 g	boneless chicken breast
10 oz	300 g	small shell pasta
1 lb	454 g	diced rapini or broccoli
2 tbsp	30 ml	herbed flavored olive oil
4	4	minced garlic cloves
1 tbsp	15 ml	chopped fresh oregano
1½ cups	375 ml	double strength chicken broth* (see page 146)
1¼ lbs	570 g	peeled, seeded and diced tomatoes
2 cups	500 ml	light cream
		Parmesan cheese to taste

Preparation:

Cut the chicken into a coarse dice.

Cook the pasta al dente in 8 cups (2 L) of boiling salted water, drain, cool.

Steam the rapini or broccoli until tender.

Brown the chicken in the olive oil in a large skillet. Sprinkle with flour, reduce the heat and cook for 2 minutes. Add the garlic, oregano, chicken broth and tomatoes sauté for 5 minutes. Add the light cream, stir in the cooked rapini or broccoli. Add the pasta and simmer 5 minutes. Serve with Parmesan cheese.

SERVES 6

* Note: Double strength broth is made by reducing broth by 50% of it's original volume, ie. 3 cups (750 ml) of chicken broth will produce 1½ cups (375 ml) double strength broth.

Chicken Broth or Stock

Ingredients:

2¼	1kg	meaty chicken bones
10 cups	2.5 L	cold water
2	2	coarsely chopped celery stalks
2	2	large, coarsely chopped carrots
1	1	coarsely chopped onion
1	1	*bouquet garni
1 tsp	5 ml	salt

Preparation:

Place the bones in a large kettle or Dutch oven.

Add the water and remaining ingredients. Simmer uncovered for 8-10 hours over very low heat.

Remove the meat (reserve and use as required), bones (discard), bouquet (discard) and vegetables (discard). Strain through a cheesecloth or fine sieve.

Chill the stock and remove any fat from the surface.

Allow stock to chill for 24 hours before using. Use for soups and sauces, or as required.

YIELDS 6 cups (1½ L)

Chef's Corner

Bouquet Garni

Bouquet Garni: tie together 2 sprigs fresh thyme, 2 sprigs marjoram, 6 peppercorns, 1 bay leaf, 6 sprigs parsley and 1 leek in a cheesecloth

Penne Beef Stroganoff

Ingredients:

2 tbsp	30 ml	safflower oil
2 tbsp	30 ml	butter
1	1	diced celery stalk
1	1	diced small onion
1	1	diced green bell pepper
1 lb	454 g	thinly sliced sirloin
3 tbsp	45 ml	all purpose flour
1½ cups	375 ml	beef broth (see page 82)
¼ cup	60 ml	sherry
½ tsp	3 ml	each of salt, pepper, paprika
1 tsp	5 ml	Dijon mustard
1 cup	250 ml	sour cream
3 cups	750 ml	penne noodles

Preparation:

In a large skillet, heat the oil and butter. Sauté the vegetables. Add the beef and sauté. Sprinkle with flour. Cook for 3 minutes.

Add the beef broth, sherry, seasonings and mustard. Reduce heat and simmer, covered for 1½ hours.

Cook the noodles in 12 cups (3 L) boiling salted water. Drain and transfer to a serving platter or bowl.

Blend the sour cream into the stroganoff mixture and mix thoroughly. Cover the noodles with stroganoff. Serve.

SERVES 4

Buckwheat Linguine
with Cheddar Velouté

Ingredients:

¾ lb	345 g	grocer purchased Buckwheat Pasta Dough or 1 quantity of our recipe *
3 tbsp	45 ml	butter
3 tbsp	45 ml	all-purpose flour
2 cups	500 ml	chicken broth (see page 146)
½ cup	125 ml	half & half cream
1 cup	250 ml	Cheddar cheese
⅓ cup	80 ml	grated Parmesan cheese

Preparation:

Process the pasta as directed and cut into linguine.

In a small saucepan melt the butter, add the flour, reduce the heat and cook for 2 minutes. Stir in the broth and cream, simmer until thick. Add the cheeses and simmer for 10 minutes.

Cook the pasta al dente in a large kettle of boiling salted water, drain. Plate the linguine and smother with the cheese sauce.

SERVES 6

* Buckwheat noodles tend to be heavy and so this recipe is suggested as an appetizer or starter to a meal rather than a meal itself.

Variation: Blend ⅓ cup (80 ml) of Cheddar cheese with 1 cup (250 ml) of Ricotta cheese and spoon this mixture over or around the pasta when serving.

Buckwheat Pasta

Ingredients:

1 cup	250 ml	buckwheat flour
½ cup	125 ml	semolina flour
1	1	extra large egg, beaten
¼ cup	60 ml	ice cold milk
		ice water, only if required

Preparation:

Blend the flours in a mixing bowl. Add the egg and milk. Knead into a smooth ball (add small amounts of ice water if required).

Knead the dough for 15 minutes and allow to rest for an additional 15 minutes. Roll out the dough. Lightly dust with flour, fold in three and roll out again. Repeat 6 to 8 times.

Now pass the dough through the pasta machine, setting the rollers gradually down until you reach the desired thickness. The result should be a smooth sheet of dough ready to process as you require.

SERVES 6

Chef's Corner

Buckwheat Pasta

When cooked, this is usually served mixed with other types of cooked pasta.

Garam Masala Mushroom
Chicken Penne

Ingredients:

3 tbsp	45 ml	olive or vegetable oil
4 oz	120 g	sliced mushrooms
¾ lb	340 g	boneless, skinless chicken breasts, cut into 1-inch cubes
½ cup	125 ml	half & half cream
2 tbsp	30 ml	chopped fresh parsley
½ tsp	3 ml	Dijon mustard with seeds
2 tsp	10 ml	Garam Masala
12 oz	340 g	penne noodles
		salt and pepper to taste

Preparation:

Heat the oil in a very large skillet over medium heat. Add the mushrooms and chicken stirring until the chicken is golden brown, about 6 minutes. Add the cream, parsley, mustard and Garam Masala to the pan and stir to remove the brown bits from the bottom and sides of the pan. Heat to boiling, reduce volume by half.

While the sauce simmers, cook the penne in 3 quarts (3 L) of boiling salted water.

Drain the pasta and transfer it to the skillet. Heat over low heat, stirring, until the penne is mixed well with the sauce. Add salt and pepper to taste; serve on hot plates.

SERVES 4

Garam Masala

Ingredients:

1 tbsp	15 ml	ground coriander
1 tbsp	15 ml	cumin
2 tsp	10 ml	ground ginger
2 tsp	10 ml	turmeric
½ tsp	3 ml	cayenne pepper
½ tsp	3 ml	black pepper
1½ tsp	8 ml	ground cardamom
¼ tsp	1 ml	ground cloves
¼ tsp	1 ml	all spice
¼ tsp	1 ml	ground bay leaves
¼ tsp	1 ml	ground nutmeg
¼ tsp	1 ml	ground cinnamon

Preparation:

Combine the spices in a spice grinder. Blend well.

Chef's Corner

Garam Masala

Garam means hot; Masala means powdered or mixture of spices. Thus, Garam Masala is a hot spice mixture. Although there are many variations of Garam Masala, we offer this one as a very good general-purpose curry powder.

Fettucini Vongolé 2

Ingredients:

1 lb	454 g	grocer purchased Pasta Verde Dough or 1 quantity of our recipe (see page110)
36	36	fresh clams
1 cup	250 ml	dry white wine
1 tbsp	15 ml	butter
2	2	minced garlic cloves
1 tbsp	15 ml	all-purpose flour
½ cup	125 ml	light cream
2 tbsp	30 ml	tomato paste
½ tsp	3 ml	salt
¼ tsp	1 ml	white pepper
1 tsp	5 ml	grated lemon rind
⅔ cup	170 ml	fresh grated Romano cheese
2 tbsp	30 ml	chopped fresh parsley

Preparation:

Prepare the pasta as directed. Cut into fettucini.

Scrub the clams and place in a saucepan, pour the wine over. Simmer gently over low heat for 6-8 minutes until the clams open, remove the clams and reserve hot. Reserve the wine.

Heat the butter in a skillet, add the garlic and sauté for 1 minute. Add the flour, reduce the heat and cook for 2 minutes, whip in the wine. Add the cream, simmer for 5 minutes. Stir in the tomato paste, seasonings and lemon rind. Simmer for an additional 3 minutes, add the reserved clams and simmer for 3 minutes.

Cook the noodles in a large kettle of salted water. Drain and place on serving plates.

Add half the Romano cheese to the sauce. Ladle the sauce over the fettucini. Sprinkle with parsley and the remaining Romano cheese and serve at once.

SERVES 6

Mandarin Chicken Fettucine

Ingredients:

1 lb	454 g	grocer purchased Basic Pasta Dough or 1 quantity of our recipe (see page 78)
1 tbsp	15 ml	butter
1	1	minced garlic clove
1 tsp	5 ml	minced ginger
1 cup	250 ml	orange juice concentrate
¼ cup	60 ml	teriyaki sauce
2 tbsp	30 ml	sherry
2 tbsp	30 ml	lime juice
12 oz	345 g	sliced, boneless, skinless chicken breasts
1 cup	250 ml	sliced water chestnuts, drained
2	2	coarsely chopped bunches watercress
3 tbsp	45 ml	lightly toasted, chopped pecans
2	2	sectioned oranges

Preparation:

Process the pasta according to directions, cut into fettuccine noodles.

In a saucepan heat the butter and sauté the garlic and ginger. Combine the orange juice, teriyaki sauce, sherry and lime juice, add to the saucepan and bring to boil. Add the chicken breasts, cover and reduce heat and simmer for 6 minutes.

Add the water chestnuts, continue to simmer for 3 minutes.

While the sauce is simmering cook the pasta in 8 cups (2 L) of boiling salted water. Drain.

In a large serving bowl, toss together the hot pasta, watercress and pecans. Arrange on serving plates. Top with the chicken mixture, smother with the sauce and serve garnished with orange segments.

SERVES 4

Orecchiette Alla Toronto

Ingredients:

2	2	red bell peppers
1 lb	454 g	hot Italian sausage meat
2 tbsp	30 ml	olive oil
1	1	large Spanish onion
2 cups	500 ml	peeled, seeded, and diced tomatoes
2 tbsp	30 ml	butter
2 tbsp	30 ml	all-purpose flour
1 cup	250 ml	milk
¼ tsp	1 ml	salt
¼ tsp	1 ml	white pepper
pinch	pinch	nutmeg
1 lb	454 g	orecchiette pasta

Preparation:

Preheat the oven to 400°F (200°C) and roast the peppers for 20 minutes. Remove from the oven and peel away the skins. Remove the core, seeds and membranes and finely dice.

In a saucepan, brown the sausage meat. Drain excess fat. Add the oil and sauté the onion until tender. Add the diced red pepper and tomatoes. Reduce heat and simmer for 30 minutes.

Melt the butter in a second saucepan. Add flour and stir into a paste (roux). Cook for 2 minutes over low heat.

Add the milk and simmer stirring until thickened. Add the seasonings and simmer 2 additional minutes.

Combine the tomato mixture with the white sauce. Simmer for 10 minutes.

While sauce simmers, cook the pasta in 8 cups (2 L) of boiling salted water for 8-9 minutes or until al dente.

Transfer pasta to serving dish and smother with sauce. Serve.

Serves 6

Basil Rigatoni
with Four Cheeses

Ingredients:

12 oz	340 g	rigatoni
2 tbsp	30 ml	butter
4 oz	120 g	shredded Bel Paese cheese
4 oz	120 g	shredded Fontina cheese
2 oz	60 g	crumbled Gorgonzola cheese
1 cup	250 ml	whipping cream
¼ cup	60 ml	chopped fresh basil
¼ cup	60 ml	fresh grated Parmesan cheese
1 tsp	5 ml	cracked black pepper
2 tbsp	30 ml	fine diced red bell peppers
2 tbsp	30 ml	fine diced yellow bell peppers

Preparation:

Cook the rigatoni in 8 cups (2 L) of boiling salted water.

While the rigatoni cooks, melt the butter in a saucepan. Add the first three cheeses stirring until melted. Blend in the cream and basil.

Place the pasta on large plate; add the sauce, tossing gently to coat.

Sprinkle with Parmesan cheese and pepper.

Garnish with red and yellow bell peppers. Serve at once.

SERVES 4

Cheese Lasagna Lite

Ingredients:

2 lbs	900 g	grocer purchased Pasta Verde Dough or 1 quantity of our recipe (see page 110)
2	2	eggs, beaten
8 oz	225 g	soy bean curd (tofu) med-soft
2 cups	500 ml	dry curd cottage cheese
1 lb	454 g	Ricotta - partly skimmed
1½ cups	375 ml	grated Romano cheese
3 cups	750 ml	Chunky Tomato Sauce

Preparation:

Prepare the pasta as directed. Roll into thin sheets. Cut the sheets into 4½ x 11 inches (11.25 x 27.50 cm). Blanch the sheets in a large kettle of boiling salted water. Drain and reserve in cold water until required.

Blend the eggs with the tofu and cheeses. Reserve ½ cup (125 ml) of Romano cheese.

In a large buttered casserole dish, place a thin layer of Chunky Tomato Sauce. Top this with a layer of noodles. Add another layer of Chunky Tomato Sauce and then a layer of cheese blend. Continue to alternate layers until complete. Be sure to finish with a layer of Chunky Tomato Sauce. Sprinkle with reserve of Romano. Cover with foil.

Bake in a 400°F (200°C) oven for 25 minutes. Remove foil and bake 8 minutes longer. Serve.

SERVES 8-10

Chunky Tomato Sauce

Ingredients:

2 tbsp	30 ml	olive oil
2	2	minced garlic cloves
1	1	diced green bell pepper
1	1	diced onion
2	2	diced celery stalks
4 oz	120 g	sliced mushrooms
1 tsp	5 ml	salt
½ tsp	3 ml	pepper
1 tsp	5 ml	basil leaves
½ tsp	3 ml	oregano leaves
½ tsp	3 ml	thyme leaves
½ tsp	3 ml	paprika
¼ tsp	1 ml	cayenne
3 lbs	1.35 kg	peeled, seeded and chopped tomatoes

Preparation:

In a sauce pan heat the oil. Sauté the garlic, green pepper, onion, celery and mushrooms until tender. Add the seasonings and tomatoes.

Simmer for 3 hours or until desired thickness. Use as required.

YIELDS 4-6 cups (1-1.5 L)

Chef's Corner

Tofu (Cheese Lasagna Lite)

Grown for many years, soy or soya beans have been a staple in both human and animal food consumption. Once, only very popular in Asian countries, soy beans advantages have now been welcomed in North America. Foods derived from soy beans are tofu (bean curd), tempeh (fermented from soy beans) and soy sauce.

Walnut Escargots Tortellini

Ingredients:

¾ lb	340 g	grocer purchased Basic Pasta Dough or ½ quantity of our recipe (see page 78)
36	36	escargots
¼ cup	60 ml	light cream
2 tbsp	30 ml	amaretto liqueur
1 cup	250 ml	skinless walnut pieces
3 tbsp	45 ml	breadcrumbs
3 tbsp	45 ml	olive oil
2	2	minced garlic cloves
3 tbsp	45 ml	chopped parsley
¼ cup	60 ml	softened butter
2 tbsp	30 ml	whipping cream
		salt & pepper to taste
		parsley sprigs
		lemon zest

Preparation:

Process the dough as directed.

Roll the dough thin. Using a 3" round cookie cutter, cut 36 rounds. Cover the rounds with a damp cloth to prevent drying.

Brush the pasta rounds with water. Place an escargot on each round. Fold and press the edges together to seal the rounds. Curl the ends around the filling and pinch together.

In 3 quarts (3 L) of boiling salted water. Cook the tortellini until they float, drain.

Heat the cream and amaretto in a saucepan, add the tortellini and simmer 3 minutes.

While the tortellini simmers, coarsely chop the nuts, place ¼ (60 ml) cup in a mixing bowl. Place the remaining nuts into a food processor along with the breadcrumbs, oil, garlic and parsley, process until smooth. Stir in the salt and pepper.

Stir in the simmered tortellini, place onto plates, pour over the cream/amaretto sauce, garnish with parsley sprigs, lemon zest and the reserved walnut pieces.

SERVES 4

Penne Alla Arrabiate

Ingredients:

¼ cup	60 ml	butter
4 oz	120 g	sliced porcini mushrooms
2	2	minced garlic cloves
2	2	diced carrots
1	1	diced onion
2	2	diced celery stalks
2 ¼ lbs	1 kg	peeled, seeded and chopped tomatoes
3	3	bay leaves
1 tsp	5 ml	thyme leaves
1 tsp	5 ml	oregano leaves
1 tsp	5 ml	basil leaves
1 tbsp	15 ml	salt
1 tsp	5 ml	pepper
1 tbsp	15 ml	crushed red chile peppers
1 lb	454 g	Penne noodles
¼ cup	60 ml	grated Parmesan cheese

Preparation:

In a large kettle, heat the butter and sauté the mushrooms, garlic, carrots, onion and celery until tender. Add the tomatoes, seasonings and chilies. Reduce heat and simmer for 3 hours.

Strain the sauce and return to the kettle, continuing to simmer until sauce is very thick.

Cook the penne in 8 cups (2 L) of boiling salted water until al dente. Put the noodles on a serving plate and smother with sauce. Sprinkle with cheese and serve.

SERVES 6

Thai Noodles

Ingredients:

3 cups	750 ml	chopped cabbage
1	1	chopped medium onion
4 tsp	20 ml	safflower oil
¼ cup	60 ml	crunchy peanut butter
1 tbsp	15 ml	fresh lime juice
4 tsp	20 ml	brown sugar
2 tsp	10 ml	soy sauce
2 tsp	10 ml	Worcestershire sauce
¼ tsp	1 ml	crushed red pepper
½ tsp	3 ml	Garam Masala powder
1	1	minced garlic clove
1	1	lemon grass stalk
1 cup	250 ml	coconut milk
1 lb	454 g	linguine noodles
1 tbsp	15 ml	chopped fresh cilantro
1 tsp	5 ml	chopped fresh basil

Preparation:

Sauté the cabbage and onion in the oil until just softened.

Add the peanut butter, lime juice, sugar, soy sauce, Worcestershire, red pepper, Garam Masala powder, garlic and lemon grass. Heat gently, adding the coconut milk gradually. Do not boil.

While sauce is simmering, cook the pasta in 8 cups (2 L) of boiling salted water until al dente, drain.

Mix the linguine with the sauce and vegetables. Mix in the cilantro and basil. Serve immediately.

SERVES 4

Salmon & Rotini Niçoise

Ingredients:

8 oz	225 g	multi-colored rotini
¾ cup	180 ml	olive oil
¼ cup	60 ml	vinegar
½ tsp	3 ml	pepper
½ tsp	3 ml	dry mustard
1 tsp	5 ml	salt
2 tbsp	30 ml	lemon juice
1	1	finely diced green onion
½ lb	225 g	blanched french cut green beans
4	4	lettuce leaves
4	4	tomatoes
4	4	hard cooked eggs
2 cups	500 ml	cooked flaked salmon
12	12	black olives, pitted
8	8	anchovy fillets
1 tbsp	15 ml	fresh basil leaves

Preparation:

Prepare the rotini according to the package directions, drain and place into a mixing bowl.

In a small mixing bowl combine the oil, vinegar, pepper, mustard, salt, and lemon juice.

Pour ¼ of the dressing over the rotini. Chill for 1 hour.

Toss the onion and beans with ¼ of the dressing.

Mix the beans into the rotini.

Place the lettuce leaves on chilled plates. Top with equal portions of salad.

Arrange equal portions of tomato, egg, salmon, olives and anchovy on top of the salad. Pour the remaining sauce over the salad. Sprinkle with basil and serve.

SERVES 4

Penne à la Rosanne

Ingredients:

2	2	yellow bell peppers
1 lb	454 g	hot Italian sausage meat
2 tbsp	30 ml	olive oil
1	1	large Spanish onion
2 cups	500 ml	peeled, seeded, and diced, tomatoes
2 tbsp	30 ml	butter
2 tbsp	30 ml	all-purpose flour
1 cup	250 ml	milk
¼ tsp	1 ml	salt
¼ tsp	1 ml	white pepper
pinch	pinch	nutmeg
1 lb	454 g	penne noodles

Preparation:

Preheat the oven to 400°F (200°C) and roast the peppers for 20 minutes. Remove from the oven and peel away the skins. Remove the cores, seeds and membranes. Dice fine.

In a sauce pan, brown the sausage meat, drain excess fat. Add the oil and sauté the onion until tender. Add the diced peppers and tomatoes. Reduce heat and simmer for 30 minutes.

Melt the butter in a second sauce pan. Add flour and stir into a paste (roux). Cook for 2 minutes over low heat.

Add the milk and stir. Simmer until thickened. Add the seasonings and simmer 2 additional minutes.

Combine the tomato mixture with the white sauce. Simmer for 10 minutes.

While sauce simmers, cook the penne in 8 cups (2L) of boiling salted water for 8-9 minutes or until al dente.

Put the pasta on a serving plate and smother with sauce. Serve.

California Gnocchi

Ingredients:

10 oz	280 g	washed fresh spinach
2 lbs	900 g	potatoes
1	1	beaten egg
1½ cups	375 ml	all-purpose flour
3 tbsp	45 ml	olive oil
3 tbsp	45 ml	all-purpose flour
⅔ cup	160 ml	chicken broth (see page 146)
⅔ cup	160 ml	light cream
⅓ cup	80 ml	tomato catsup
2 tsp	10 ml	Worcestershire sauce
1 tsp	5 ml	paprika
3 drops	3 drops	Tabasco™ sauce
1 tbsp	15 ml	lemon juice

Preparation:

Steam the spinach. Cool. Chop or process until very fine.

Pare the potatoes then steam in a large kettle until they are fork tender. Drain well. Purée. Blend in the spinach. Place in a mixing bowl. Add the egg and 1 cup (250 ml) of flour. Knead the dough adding more flour as required. The dough should be firm yet soft.

Mold 1 tsp (5 ml) of mixture on a spoon. Roll gently in your hands. (Be sure to flour your hands.) Place on a lightly floured surface and press with a fork.

Cook the gnocchi in a large kettle of salted boiling water. Once they float cook for an additional 3 minutes.

While the gnocchi cooks, heat the oil in a sauce pan, add the 3 tbsp (45 ml) of flour and cook for 2 minutes over low heat. Whisk in the broth and cream and simmer until thick.

Whisk in the remaining ingredients, continue to simmer for 2 additional minutes.

Drain the gnocchi and place in a large serving bowl, smother with the sauce and serve.

SERVES 6

Shrimp Capellini

Ingredients:

10 oz	300 g	grocer purchased Tomato Pasta Dough or ½ quantity of our recipe (see page 98)
3 tbsp	45 ml	olive oil
3 tbsp	45 ml	all-purpose flour
⅔ cup	160 ml	chicken broth (see page 146)
⅔ cup	160 ml	light cream
⅓ cup	80 ml	tomato catsup
2 tsp	10 ml	Worcestershire sauce
1 tsp	5 ml	paprika
3 drops	3 drops	Tabasco™ sauce
1 tbsp	15 ml	lemon juice
3 oz	80 g	freshly grated Romano cheese
2 cups	500 ml	small cooked fresh water shrimp

Preparation:

Process the dough according to the directions, cut into capellini noodles.

Heat the oil in a saucepan, add the flour and cook for 2 minutes over low heat. Whisk in the broth and cream, simmer until thick.

Whisk in the remaining ingredients except the shrimp, continue to simmer for 2 additional minutes.

Cook the pasta in 4 cups (1 L) of boiling salted water until al dente.

Toss the pasta with the sauce, sprinkle with the shrimp and serve.

SERVES 4.

Chicken Cashew Double Wong

Ingredients:

¾ lb	340 g	grocer purchased Egg Pasta Dough or 1 quantity of our recipe (see page 122)
4 tbsp	60 ml	peanut oil
1 lb	454 g	diced chicken
¼ cup	60 ml	unsalted cashew nuts
¼ lb	115 g	shrimp
½ cup	125 ml	diced celery
½ cup	125 ml	diced onion
½ cup	125 ml	sliced mushrooms
½ cup	125 ml	diced green peppers
2 tbsp	30 ml	unsalted peanut butter
2 tbsp	30 ml	soy sauce
2 tbsp	30 ml	sherry
1 tbsp	15 ml	honey

Preparation:

In a kettle cook the noodles. Drain and reserve.

In a wok or large skillet heat the oil. Quickly fry the chicken, cashews, shrimp and the vegetables until chicken is thoroughly cooked.

Add the noodles. Fry one side and then turn over and fry the other.

Blend the peanut butter, soy sauce, sherry and honey. Pour over noodles. Cook 1 minute and transfer to a serving platter. Serve at once.

SERVES 6

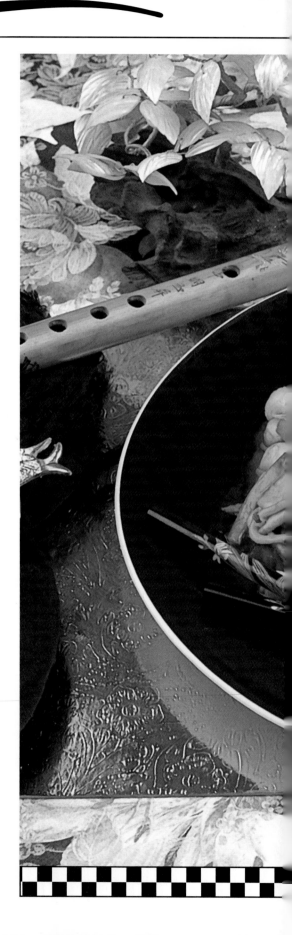

Expresso Cannoli

Ingredients:

⅓ cup	80 ml	hot water
3 tbsp	45 ml	instant coffee crystals
1	1	egg
2 cups	500 ml	all-purpose flour
4 cups	1 L	safflower oil
¼ cup	60 ml	confectioners' sugar
½ tsp	3 ml	vanilla extract
2 tbsp	30 ml	candied orange zest
2 tbsp	30 ml	chocolate chips
2 tbsp	30 ml	chopped pistachio nuts
2 cups	500 ml	Mascarpone cheese
2 cups	500 ml	Coffee Chocolate Sauce
1 cup	250 ml	sweetened whipped cream
½ cup	125 ml	fresh raspberries
		mint leaves for garnish

Preparation:

Dissolve the coffee crystals in the water. Cool. Beat the egg and blend in the coffee. Add the flour and knead into a smooth ball. Roll the dough out and lightly dust with the flour, fold into thirds. Repeat rolling, dusting with the flour and folding 6-8 times or until the dough is firm. Roll the dough very thin and cut into 2" (5 cm) squares.

Roll the squares around a cannoli tube or a dowel.

Heat the oil to 375°F (190°C). Deep fry the cannoli until crisp, remove from the oil, drain on absorbent paper and cool to room temperature.

In a mixing bowl blend the sugar, vanilla, orange zest, chocolate chips, pistachio nuts and Mascarpone cheese. Fill the cooled cannoli with the cheese mixture.

Ladle a small amount of the Coffee Chocolate Sauce over a serving plate, place the cannoli on top of the sauce. Pipe a small amount of whipped cream on to the cannoli, sprinkle with raspberries and garnish with mint leaves. Serve at once.

SERVES 4

Coffee Chocolate Sauce

Ingredients:

1 cup	250 ml	boiling water
2 tsp	10 ml	instant coffee crystals
2 tbsp	30 ml	sugar
4	4	egg yolks
⅓ cup	80 ml	whipping cream
1½ tsp	8 ml	cornstarch
2 tbsp	30 ml	milk
2 oz	60 g	chocolate chips

Preparation:

Dissolve the coffee crystals in the boiling water. Place in a double boiler. Add the sugar and stir until dissolved. Whip in the egg yolks one at a time. Add the cream and cook for 2 minutes.

Mix the cornstarch into the milk. Add to the sauce along with the chocolate. Gently cook until sauce thickens. Remove from the heat. Use as required.

YIELDS 2 cups (500 ml)

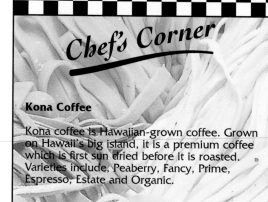

Chef's Corner

Kona Coffee

Kona coffee is Hawaiian-grown coffee. Grown on Hawaii's big island, it is a premium coffee which is first sun dried before it is roasted. Varieties include, Peaberry, Fancy, Prime, Espresso, Estate and Organic.

Orecchiette
with Radicchio, Ham & Cream

Ingredients:

1 lb	454 g	grocer purchased Cornmeal Pasta or 1 quantity of our recipe (see page 114)
2 tbsp	30 ml	butter
4 oz	120 g	julienne sliced ham
2 cups	500 ml	heavy cream
1 cup	250 ml	freshly grated Parmesan cheese
2 tsp	10 ml	cracked black pepper
2 cups	500 ml	julienne sliced radicchio

Preparation:

To make orecchiette (little ears) divide the pasta in half. Roll into a long rope shape and cut into ⅛" (3 mm) thick rounds. Dust each with flour. Place a round in the palm of your hand and indent the centre with your finger. Repeat until all rounds are complete.

In a large kettle of boiling salted water drop the orecchiette into the water. Once the orecchiette floats to the top, cook for an additional 3 minutes. Place onto a warm serving plate.

Heat the butter in a skillet. Sauté the ham for 1 minute. Add the cream and reduce by ⅓ rd. Stir in the Parmesan cheese and pepper. Pour over the orecchiette. Toss in the radicchio. Plate and serve.

SERVES 4

Beef Fusili

Ingredients:

3 tbsp	45 ml	olive oil
1 lb	454 g	beef tenderloin diced in ½" (1.25 cm) cubes
1	1	sliced onion
¼ cup	60 ml	finely diced green bell peppers
¼ cup	60 ml	finely diced red bell peppers
1	1	finely diced celery stalk
4 oz	120 g	button mushrooms
1 tsp	5 ml	ground Hungarian paprika
½ tsp	3 ml	dried thyme leaves
½ tsp	3 ml	dried basil leaves
½ tsp	3 ml	dried oregano leaves
½ tsp	3 ml	salt
½ tsp	3 ml	cracked pepper
1 tsp	5 ml	Worcestershire sauce
¼ cup	60 ml	sherry
3 cups	750 ml	Marinara Sauce
1 lb	454 g	fusili noodles

Preparation:

In a large skillet heat the oil. Brown the tenderloin. Add the onion, bell peppers, celery and mushrooms and sauté until tender. Sprinkle with the seasonings.

Add the Worcestershire, sherry and Marinara Sauce, reduce heat and simmer 15 minutes.

In a large kettle of boiling salted water, cook the pasta al dente. Drain and place the fusili on serving plates. Ladle generous amounts of the beef sauce over the fusili. Serve.

SERVES 6

Marinara Sauce

Ingredients:

3	3	red cascabel chilies
⅓ cup	80 ml	chopped black olives
2 tbsp	30 ml	capers
⅓ cup	80 ml	olive oil
1	1	finely diced onion
2	2	minced garlic cloves
1½ lbs	675 g	peeled, seeded and chopped tomatoes
2 tsp	10 ml	oregano leaves

Preparation:

Seed and dice the chilies, then mix with the olives, capers and half of the oil. Marinate for 1 hour.

Heat the remaining oil in a saucepan. Sauté the onion and garlic until tender.

Drain the marinade and mix with the onion. Add the tomatoes and the oregano. Reduce heat to medium. Cook until sauce has thickened. Serve over pasta.

YIELDS 3 cups (750 ml)

Chef's Corner

Button mushrooms

Button mushrooms are the world's most common and most cultivated mushrooms. They are generally sold fresh in your grocer's produce section. Look for the mushrooms with the round button-like head. Their proper name is "Agaricus bisporus". It is by far easier to remember "button mushrooms".

Beef with Chinese Mushroom

Ingredients:

½ lb	225 g	flank steak
3 tbsp	45 ml	peanut oil
½ tsp	3 ml	baking soda
2	2	minced garlic cloves
2 tsp	10 ml	granulated sugar
1 tsp	5 ml	salt
3 tbsp	45 ml	light soy sauce
2 tbsp	30 ml	white wine
6	6	dried Chinese mushroom, soak 1 hr. in warm water
¾ lb	340 g	grocer purchased Egg Pasta noodles or 1 quantity of our recipe (see page 122)

SAUCE:

2 tbsp	30 ml	dark soy sauce
2 tbsp	30 ml	sherry
1	1	minced garlic clove
1 tsp	5 ml	minced ginger
4 tbsp	60 ml	oyster sauce
1 tsp	5 ml	cornstarch
1 tbsp	15 ml	water
		Sliced tomatoes for garnish

Preparation:

Trim the beef of any fat and cut in thin strips.

Blend 1 tbsp (15 ml) of oil, baking soda, garlic, sugar, salt, soy and white wine. Slice steak thin and place in a mixing bowl. Pour the marinade over and marinate for 20 minutes. Drain beef.

Drain and slice the mushrooms.

Blend the dark soy, sherry, garlic, ginger and oyster sauce.

Cook the noodles in salted boiling water, drain and reserve.

Heat the remaining oil in a wok. Quickly fry the beef, add the mushrooms and continue to cook for 3 minutes. Add the noodles and continue to cook for 2 minutes. Stir in the sauce and cook 1 additional minute. Mix the cornstarch with the water and add to the noodles, reduce heat and simmer until thick. Serve with tomatoes for garnish.

SERVES 4

Beef'N Macaroni

Ingredients:

2 tbsp	30 ml	safflower oil
1 lb	454 g	lean beef cut into 1" (2.5 cm) cubes
½	0.5	chopped large onion
2	2	coarse diced carrots
1	1	coarse diced celery stalk
1	1	sweet red pepper cut into ½" (1.25 cm) strips
8 oz	225 g	small button mushrooms, brushed
1 cup	250 ml	stewed tomatoes
1 cup	250 ml	red wine
1	1	bay leaf
1 tbsp	15 ml	fresh thyme
1 tsp	5 ml	Worcestershire sauce
2 tbsp	30 ml	dark soy sauce
2 tbsp	30 ml	tomato paste
¼ cup	60 ml	chopped fresh parsley
¼ tsp	1 ml	hot red pepper flakes
8 oz	225 g	elbow macaroni, small penne, ziti or radiatore
½ tsp	3 ml	salt
¼ tsp	1 ml	black pepper
1 cup	250 ml	frozen peas, thawed

Preparation:

In a large heavy pot heat the oil, add the beef and fry until brown. Add the onion, carrots, celery, red pepper, mushrooms, tomatoes, wine, bay leaf, thyme, Worcestershire, soy sauce, tomato paste, parsley and red pepper flakes. Cover and simmer over low heat for 1½ hours, stirring occasionally.

Process the pasta according to the package directions. Drain and add to the stew. Stir in the salt, and pepper, cover and cook an additional 10 minutes, stirring occasionally. Add the peas and stir to mix. Serve hot.

SERVES 6

Oriental Beef and Tomato on Noodle.

Ingredients:

½ tsp	3 ml	baking soda
3 tbsp	45 ml	peanut oil
2	2	minced garlic cloves
2 tsp	10 ml	sugar
1 tsp	5 ml	salt
3 tbsp	45 ml	soy sauce
2 tbsp	30 ml	sherry
1 lb	454 g	flank steak
4 oz	120 g	button mushrooms
1	1	sliced medium onion
1 cup	250 ml	peeled, seeded, chopped tomatoes
1 tsp	5 ml	cornstarch
1 tbsp	15 ml	water
12 oz	345 g	Chinese noodles

Preparation:

Blend the baking soda with 1 tbsp (15 ml) of oil, the garlic, sugar, salt, soy sauce and sherry. Thinly slice the steak and place in a large mixing bowl. Pour marinade over beef and set aside for 20 minutes.

In a large wok or skillet, heat the remaining oil. Drain the beef and reserve the marinade. Fry the beef, mushrooms and onion for 3 minutes. Add the reserved marinade and tomatoes. Reduce heat and simmer for 1 minute. Mix the cornstarch with the water and add to the beef. Simmer until sauce thickens.

While cooking the beef, cook the noodles in a large kettle of boiling salted water. Drain and transfer to a large platter. Pour beef over the noodles and serve.

SERVES 6

About the Author

Mr. Kalenuik, affectionately known as Chef K (by those who could not pronounce his last name), began his culinary career in Jasper Alberta, Canada, in 1973 at the world famous Jasper Park Lodge. Since then, he has established himself as Chef de Cuisine in many of the finer restaurants and hotels throughout Canada.

Ron has owned and operated several award winning restaurants. He is a teacher and consultant to the hospitality industry as well as President of the North American Institute of Modern Cuisine Inc.

As an author, he expresses a unique and creative flair in all areas of cookery. Whether classic or just down home family cookery, or in modern presentation, every style is simply given and easily prepared. This book is more than a collection of recipes; it is a collection of useable, delicious recipes that will become a standard in anyone's kitchen, from the homemaker to the professional chef.

With *The Original Pizza & Pasta Cookbook*, Mr. Kalenuik's career includes 10 cookery books to date. His international best selling series of *Simply Delicious Cooking* has sold over 2,500,000 copies the world over. His other books include *International Family Favorites, The Fundamentals of Taste, Cuisine Extraordinaire, Dining In, Championship Cooking, Chef K's Cheese Best* and *The Right Spice*.

A Word from the Author

e cooking passions of people run deep, whether they are in the latest trend or "just doing what om always did." People hold onto what they know works for them. That is why the *Simply licious Cooking* series is so important to more than 2,500,000 people. These are cookbooks they ow they can hold onto, and trust for success in their kitchens. Now you, too, can enjoy that liance with *The Original Pizza & Pasta Cookbook.*

ost want the best for their families and they deserve it. This is what we bring you in *The Original zza & Pasta Cookbook,* the best in simple and delightful recipes. No matter where you live these e sure to provide your family with exactly what you want for them: the very best.

ιe best cooks are the ones who are always seeking inspiration, looking to marry the old with the w so that creativity may flow. In *The Original Pizza & Pasta Cookbook,* the inspiration is defined .d perfected. There is no recipe too hard or so different that one will pass it by. Every recipe has e taste of "just one more bite" leaving the guest with an immense desire for a new summons to e table.

ɔ cook can resist the draw of his or her favorite recipes; nor could I. I've brought to you eations that have won awards and rave reviews from friends and critics alike. I've given to you ɔre than just years of cooking experience. I've given you the tastes of culinary dreams. I hope ɔu'll live the dream with me.

ɔm my first international best-selling cookery book *Simply Delicious Cooking,* I learned that my aders sought more international cuisine. We have answered the call, for within these pages ɔu'll find cuisine from Africa to Asian New Zealand to Newfoundland, from the U.S.A. to the K. and points between.

ith *The Original Pizza & Pasta Cookbook,* we seek to give you years of enjoyment in food eparation. After all, food should be a pleasure to prepare and serve. This is accomplished here. ιste is the complete work of all the senses, not just the mouth, with all the senses working gether for your enjoyment. To make the best use of taste, one must incorporate sight, touch, ιell, hearing and flavor to yield taste. Here I have accomplished this for you; our pictures are ιt a prelude to the tastes that will follow. they are the appetizers for the eyes.

ɔur book looks like a coffee table book, something for show. However, beautiful as it is, it really ·longs in the kitchen where your most reliable cooking tools are. Open the pages to a new world international delights that could change your world of culinary abilities forever.

Ron Kalenuik, Chef K

Index

Index

Index